Medicaid Reform

Medicaid Reform
Four Studies
of Case Management

Deborah A. Freund
with Polly M. Ehrenhaft
and Marie Hackbarth

American Enterprise Institute for Public Policy Research
Washington and London

Deborah Freund is a professor of economics at the University of North Carolina. Polly Ehrenhaft is a Washington-based health policy analyst. Marie Hackbarth is a research associate at AEI.

This volume was prepared under a grant from the J.M. Foundation of New York.

Library of Congress Cataloging in Publication Data

Freund, Deborah A.
  Medicaid Reform.

  I. Medicaid—Case studies. I. Ehrenhaft, Polly. II. Hackbarth, Marie. III. Title.
HD7102.U4F68 1984   353.9'3841045   84-11058
ISBN 0-8447-3561-2

AEI Studies 408

Printed in the United States of America

Contents

LIST OF TABLES

Foreword

This volume—made possible by a grant from the J.M. Foundation of New York—carries on work that began two years ago, when AEI's Center for Health Policy Research visited ten Medicaid experiments that were just getting under way. AEI published short case studies of each one in *Restructuring Medicaid: State and Local Initiatives*, which was also funded by the J.M. Foundation.

The present volume offers case studies in greater detail of four Medicaid initiatives. Three of them—in Michigan, in Kentucky, and in Santa Barbara County, California—were first described in *Restructuring Medicaid*; now they are examined more fully a year later, after they have been operating for a while. The fourth initiative—in Utah—is new to this book.

The initiatives studied here are representative of efforts being made in a growing majority of states to institute some system of case management for Medicaid recipients. By making individual physicians responsible for "managing" each recipient's care, these models aim to control unnecessary expenditures even while improving access to and the continuity of care for Medicaid beneficiaries.

The programs conducted by AEI's Center for Health Policy Research have focused on issues in the forefront of public debate. In *Market Reforms in Health Care* (1983), edited by Jack A. Meyer, the center's director, we explored some of the key decisions to be made and the barriers to be overcome in implementing a system of incentives for cost-conscious choices in health care. In *Passing the Health Care Buck* (1983), Jack Meyer examined the controversial question of the "cost shift" from public to private payers of hospital bills. And in *Managing Health Care Costs* (1984), also funded by the J.M. Foundation, Sean Sullivan studied private sector innovations in cost containment. This volume looks more closely at state Medicaid reforms that are taking public policy in new directions.

WILLIAM J. BAROODY, JR.
President
American Enterprise Institute

Preface

Medicaid—jointly funded by the federal government and the states—is at a critical juncture. A combination of reduced real-dollar federal assistance to the states and soaring health care costs is putting state governments in a tightening vise. Balanced budget requirements leave states with only three ways to escape from this squeeze: (1) by cutting back Medicaid benefits and eligibility; (2) by cutting other program expenditures for services such as education and transportation; or (3) by devising workable reforms in the health care payment and delivery systems that will enable governments to serve Medicaid eligibles adequately and at a more affordable cost.

The financing reforms examined in this volume try to choose the third way. They hold the promise of averting further cutbacks in eligibility and further restrictions on covered health services. They may also keep us off a fiscal seesaw on which health costs soar while programs to meet other human needs sink.

In this book the case studies of new Medicaid initiatives assess both the promise and the problems associated with introducing reforms based on incentives for cost-conscious behavior. They examine the barriers to implementation of these reforms and suggest ways to surmount these barriers. Issues such as the proper degree of risk that providers of health care should shoulder, the design of programs to ensure quality, the establishment of grievance procedures, and the proper administration and management of the programs are explored here.

Examination of growing pains and problems and of successful techniques for addressing them should be useful not only to other state and local governments pondering how to manage Medicaid costs but also to the private sector. As business and labor experiment with cost-management techniques that resemble the programs studied here, they too can benefit from lessons the states are learning.

The initiatives described in this book are typically pilot projects operating in selected counties of each state. Some may grow into statewide programs or be copied in other states, while others—like Citicare in Kentucky—will falter for various reasons. Our purpose is not to promote any specific model of payment system reform, but to explore the ingredients of success and failure.

Inasmuch as these programs are new and experimental, many of the conclusions drawn in this study are tentative. By scrutinizing these programs at their embryonic stages, however, we hope to elucidate the process of program development and help other public and private sector participants in health care markets find ways to contain costs while preserving access to good-quality health care.

JACK A. MEYER

1
Overview: Efforts to Cap the Costs of Medicaid

Medicaid is a combined federal-state program providing health care benefits to low-income households. The total cost of the program has risen sharply in recent years, as have all health care costs, and it is expected to continue rising in the future. Expenditures for Medicaid, including federal and state contributions, have increased from $14.1 billion in 1975 to $34 billion in 1982 and are projected to reach $40.7 billion in 1984.

Growing concern about federal budget deficits and about the sustained growth in entitlement programs has placed more and more pressure on the Medicaid program to contain costs. Interestingly, though, Medicaid costs have not risen nearly as rapidly as Medicare costs: the average annual rate of increase in Medicaid costs from 1975 to 1982 was 13.3 percent, whereas the corresponding rate of increase for Medicare was 18.1 percent.

The attempts of the federal and state governments to reduce the increase in Medicaid costs have been primarily directed at reducing the benefit package, limiting eligibility, increasing utilization controls, or freezing rates for provider reimbursement. Although these changes have tempered the pace of Medicaid cost increases, they have still left most state governments and the federal government with a significant problem in containing health care costs.

There is evidence that Medicaid has significantly improved the health of the poor. The proportion of the poor *eligible* for Medicaid benefits, however, has declined since the mid-1970s, and currently only about half of the individuals below the poverty line are eligible. Moreover, many states have reduced covered services for those households that *are* eligible. We cannot continue to reduce Medicaid services or eligibility without jeopardizing the gains that have been made in improving the health of the poor.

In recent years, the Reagan administration and Congress have emphasized finding solutions to the structural problems inherent in the Medicaid delivery systems and deemphasized palliatives that result only in temporary gains. The realization that previous approaches to cost containment either have been ineffective or are no longer politically acceptable has prompted many states to restructure their Medicaid programs under waivers granted by the Health Care Financing Administration (HCFA) of the U.S. Department of Health and Human Services. Research has found, for example, that utilization review, peer review, and certificate-of-need programs have had little effect in containing health care costs.[1] Even statewide rate-setting programs, which have frequently produced savings of 1 to 2 percent, cannot guarantee enough cost savings to make the Medicaid program solvent. States have consequently been forced to look elsewhere for solutions to increasing Medicaid costs, and many are looking more toward market-oriented solutions to the problem.[2]

This book presents four case studies of communities that have attempted to increase access to health care for Medicaid beneficiaries as well as to reduce the rate of increase in Medicaid costs through a market-oriented (competitive) approach. The sites that were surveyed are Wayne County, Michigan; Salt Lake, Weber, and Utah counties, Utah; Jefferson County, Kentucky; and Santa Barbara County, California. These particular sites were selected because they are geographically diverse, they had not been part of a major evaluation by the federal government at the time of this writing,[3] they had an innovative approach to implementing a more competitive model, and they were diverse in organizational form or sponsorship. We excluded sites concentrating on long-term care in favor of those dealing with hospitals and physicians. Though critically important, the financing of long-term care is sufficiently different in organization and complexity to warrant a separate study.

This book focuses on problems program administrators faced in effecting structural changes and the strategies they developed to establish the programs and to enroll patients. Although the communities studied differed in several respects, we tried to identify the

---

1. Bruce Steinwald and Frank A. Sloan, "Regulatory Approaches to Hospital Cost Containment: A Synthesis of the Empirical Evidence," in *A New Approach to the Economics of Health Care* (Washington, D.C.: American Enterprise Institute, 1981), pp. 273-307.

2. Alain Enthoven, *Health Plan: The Only Practical Solution to the Soaring Cost of Medical Care* (Reading, Mass.: Addison Wesley, 1980).

3. A continuing evaluation of the Santa Barbara Health Authority is being conducted by a consortium of researchers from the Research Triangle Institute, the University of North Carolina at Chapel Hill, the Medical College of Virginia, the American Enterprise Institute, and Lewin and Associates under contract with the Health Care Financing Administration.

implementation problems common to all sites so that specific strategies could be devised for resolving the problems in other communities.

Much of the information presented in this book is the result of interviews conducted at each site. Among those interviewed were legislators, state employees, hospital administrators, hospital-based and private practice physicians, public health officers, and actuaries. Their contributions are gratefully acknowledged.

The case studies are presented in the order in which the programs were implemented; they are also in order from the least change in the Medicaid program to the greatest. Information presented on each site is current through the dates on which the interviews were conducted: for Michigan, January 1983; for Utah, August 1983; for Kentucky, June 1984; and for California, September 1983.

The following chapters explore in detail the specific programs at the four sites. This chapter explains some of the factors that influenced the development of the various programs, including the political environment and the support from constituency groups. It also discusses eligibility and enrollment issues, program administration, and remuneration and risk sharing for providers, including hospitals and physicians. To place the analysis in context, this chapter first sets out the legislative background to the demonstration programs.

Legislative Background to the Demonstration Programs

States must design and manage their Medicaid programs in accordance with certain federal statutory requirements. These requirements define the types of care reimbursable by the federal government through its matching payments to the states. But in recognition that state Medicaid programs may want to test new approaches to the delivery and financing of services to beneficiaries, the Medicaid law provides that compliance with these requirements may be waived to allow states to carry out demonstration projects.

Section 1115 of the Social Security Act permits the administrator of the HCFA to waive statutory requirements to enable a state to carry out any experimental pilot and demonstration project that in his or her judgment would be likely to assist in promoting competition. The administrator's approval of such waivers is contingent on the development of a detailed research methodology and a comprehensive evaluation plan for the demonstration. State applications to conduct demonstration projects are also subject to public inspection and comment. No time limit is set for the administrator to act on state waiver requests.

3

Section 2175 (part 1915) of the Omnibus Reconciliation Act of 1981 and the Medicare and Medicaid Amendments of 1981 streamlined the waiver process and broadened the scope of the waivers. The secretary of health and human services can now waive requirements of Medicaid law to enable states to carry out competitive programs under Medicaid without developing a formal demonstration project. The research and evaluation criteria required for demonstrations under the previous law no longer apply. States will only be expected to document the cost effectiveness of the waiver and its effect on the program. Approval of a waiver request will also be contingent on a state's ability to show that the program will not substantially impair access to services of high quality.

Both the section 2175 and the section 1115 waiver authorities permit states to contract for service with selective providers or to experiment with alternative delivery systems. To the extent that the secretary or the administrator of the HCFA finds it to be cost effective and efficient, he or she may waive such requirements of Medicaid law to enable a state to:

• implement a case management system that restricts the provider from whom an individual eligible for Medicaid can obtain primary care services (other than in an emergency), if such a restriction does not substantially impair access to services of adequate quality where medically necessary

• share with Medicaid recipients, through direct payment or additional services, any cost savings resulting from their use of more cost-effective delivery systems, such as health maintenance organizations (HMOs)

• act as broker in giving Medicaid recipients a choice of competing health care plans, if such a restriction does not substantially impair access to services of adequate quality where medically necessary

• place restrictions on providers or practitioners from or through which a Medicaid recipient may obtain services (other than emergency services), provided that (1) such providers or practitioners accept and comply with the reimbursement, quality, and utilization standards under the state plan; (2) such restrictions are consistent with access, quality, and efficient and economic provision of care and services; and (3) such restrictions do not discriminate among classes of providers on grounds unrelated to their demonstrated effectiveness and efficiency in providing services

The new Medicaid law also provides that a state will not be held out of compliance for failure to meet certain statutory requirements if it:

4

- "locks in" beneficiaries who overutilize services to a particular provider for a reasonable time
- "locks out" providers who abuse the program, subject to prior notice and opportunity for a hearing and provided that eligible individuals have reasonable access to services of adequate quality

The legislative intent of these Medicaid amendments is to promote efficiency and effectiveness in the delivery of services to Medicaid beneficiaries. The potential advantages of a case management system in providing coordinated and comprehensive care to Medicaid beneficiaries and limiting providers to those with demonstrated ability to provide effective and efficient care are believed to justify the restriction on beneficiaries' freedom of choice on a demonstration basis.

Waiver of the requirement for statewide effectiveness of state Medicaid programs is seen as necessary to ensure that a state will not be precluded from entering into economical arrangements with competing health plans even though it is unable to enter into comparable arrangements statewide. The legislative intent of this waiver authority is also to ensure that access to quality health care services that are sufficient to meet the genuine needs of all Medicaid recipients be maintained and that such services be available from enough providers in enough locations to be reasonably accessible to all recipients. Waiver authority is contingent on the determination that the restrictions placed on recipients by a demonstration project will not substantially impair access to services of adequate quality.

The Medicare and Medicaid Amendments of 1981 also allowed for greater flexibility in participation of HMOs and prepaid providers in state Medicaid programs. Medicaid had previously allowed state Medicaid plans to enter into risk-based payment arrangements with HMOs, but few states had taken advantage of this provision. The current waiver authority allows state Medicaid plans to act as central brokers in giving Medicaid recipients a choice of competing health plans such as HMOs and to share with Medicaid recipients any cost savings resulting from their use of those plans. The new Medicaid provisions aim to encourage HMOs to participate in the Medicaid program because of their demonstrated cost effectiveness.

Under previous Medicaid law, states could enter into prepaid capitation or other risk-based arrangements only with HMOs that are federally qualified under title VIII of the Public Health Service Act. The new Medicaid provisions permit states to contract with HMOs that are not federally qualified if they offer the same services available to persons eligible for Medicaid who are not enrolled in the HMO and make provisions against the risk of insolvency to ensure that enrollees under

5

the contracts are not held liable for payment for services received under the contract.

Under previous Medicaid law, most HMOs participating in state Medicaid programs were prohibited from having persons eligible for Medicaid and Medicare constitute half or more of their enrollment. Recognizing that in some areas, even with a three-year compliance period, the 50 percent limit on Medicare and Medicaid enrollment may be unrealistic, the new law raises the ceiling on combined Medicare and Medicaid enrollment to 75 percent (to be achieved within three years of the initiation of the contract between the HMO and the state). The secretary may modify or waive this ceiling for an HMO for such a period as deemed appropriate if special circumstances such as the high proportion of Medicare and Medicaid beneficiaries in the HMO's service area warrant and if the HMO is making reasonable efforts to enroll non-Medicare and non-Medicaid members.

Under previous law, if a Medicaid beneficiary enrolled in an HMO in one month and shortly thereafter lost his or her eligibility for benefits because of excess income, the HMO was denied payment for services provided after the individual became ineligible. Recognizing that, from the HMO's standpoint, this provision made the Medicaid market unstable and therefore unattractive, the new Medicaid law authorizes, but does not require, states to negotiate an enrollment period of up to six months for persons eligible for Medicaid who elect to enroll in an HMO, with the assurance that federal matching funds will be available for the HMO coverage during that period. This guarantee of a six-month enrollment applies only to persons who involuntarily lose Medicaid eligibility. (In general, the six-month period is not renewable.) The waivers granted to each state are shown in table 1.

The Political Environment and Constituency Support

The programs in Michigan, Utah, Kentucky, and California are each organized differently, and each program has a different type of sponsorship. In Michigan, the state legislature saw no alternatives for containing costs and, as a result, passed legislation that challenged providers to develop cost-saving strategies of their own. The plan eventually chosen was designed by the Michigan State Medical Society and the Michigan Association of Osteopathic Physicians and Surgeons. Hence, physicians, legislators, and state government quickly and easily accepted the Primary Physician Sponsor Program (PPSP).

Initially consumer groups, such as welfare rights organizations, were excluded from planning the PPSP, and they complained bitterly. In response to these complaints, the planning process was restruc-

TABLE 1

WAIVERS OF THE SOCIAL SECURITY ACT, BY STATE

	Michigan	Utah	California	Kentucky
Section 1902 (a) (1) (statewideness)	X	X	X	X
Section 1902 (a) (10) (amount, duration, and scope)				X
Section 1902 (a) (23) (freedom of choice)	X	X	X	X
Section 1902 (a) (13), (a) (30), (a) (4) (flexibility in reimbursement agreements)			X	
Section 1902 (a) (30), (a) (33a) (case management utilization review plan)			X	
2175 authority	X	X		X
1915 (b) (1) case management	X	X		X
1915 (b) (3) shared cost savings		X		
1915 (b) (4) restrict providers (for example, contract for laboratory and pharmacy)				X
1115 authority			X	

SOURCE: Author.

tured to permit more consumer participation, and an evaluation of consumer attitudes was funded through a welfare rights coalition. The welfare rights coalition also provides a hotline service and takes patients' grievances to the state. Thus the state expanded the political support from Medicaid recipients for its program.

The Utah Choice of Health Care Program is a better example of a program that formed a basis of support for itself by cultivating the endorsement of important constituencies in the state. Prior endorsement of a more competitive initiative by the governor, the legislature, and the Department of Health made the development of the Choice plan even easier. Although the plan is to be administered solely by the state, both the medical society and the welfare rights groups were informed of the program in its early stages. (The medical society had initially endorsed the program; however, it withdrew its endorsement at a later date.) Community support was crucial in planning how to educate enrollees about the system and in developing information about the program.

Kentucky's Citicare program grew out of a much different political environment. Citicare resulted from a funding crisis at University

7

Hospital in Louisville, which had been the primary source of care for Medicaid beneficiaries. Task forces—including state government, county government, and the private sector but excluding consumers and state legislators—were appointed to find solutions to the problem. A decision was finally made to form a private, not-for-profit corporation to run Citicare and to contract with an independent fiscal agent for the administration of the plan. The program was implemented quickly and decisively but without the participation of local community groups or consumers and without the endorsement of the Jefferson County or Fall City (in Louisville) medical society.

The last program discussed here is the Santa Barbara Special Health Care Authority, which was created independent of county government to administer the Santa Barbara Health Initiative. The Health Initiative was formed despite the reluctance of the state and of certain specialists in the medical community. After the initial physician enrollment period, no ophthalmologists, orthopedists, or neurosurgeons were signed up with the Health Initiative. Nevertheless, the clientele appeared generally satisfied, probably because of consumer participation on the board of directors.

Although enlisting the support of every interest group may not be necessary, community support appears very important to the success of such programs, especially during implementation. Most programs studied, however, were planned by a small group of responsible individuals from state government who had little time to consider the concerns expressed by certain constituencies or to take cognizance of their own position on the issues.

Apparently the support of physicians or the medical society also makes implementation easier. It is almost impossible to satisfy a broad range of interests, such as those of providers and hospital administrators, or to allay the fears of people who wish to continue with "business as usual." Nevertheless, medical societies have provided their support and, in many instances, their sponsorship for these programs because the programs provide access to health care—through a primary care physician—for those who have not previously had access, and because an increase in payments to participating physicians frequently results.

Eligibility and Enrollment

Any restructuring effort in the Medicaid program requires close coordination of the eligibility and enrollment systems. This coordination is often difficult because Medicaid and welfare eligibility are traditionally controlled by the state's social service department whereas enrollment is controlled by the health department or by the sponsor of the demonstration program. The cooperation, coordination, and reeducation of individuals responsible for eligibility and enrollment are crucial if the plan involves prepayment. States must design computer programs to ensure that only those who are eligible will be in the program and that health plans are paid for precisely those persons. Failure to perform enrollment on a daily basis or to merge eligibility and enrollment will cause overpayment to some plans and underpayment to others, retroactive denial of payment, angry providers, and program failure.

Eligibility and enrollment responsibilities in each of the programs are handled by different agencies and with varying degrees of success.

In Michigan both eligibility determination and enrollment procedures are supervised by the Department of Social Services, but by different sections of the department. The department has hired ten former case workers to supervise enrollment. Eligibility is determined by yet a different group of social workers. Dividing responsibility has meant that though experienced with the Medicaid program and populations, enrollment workers cannot provide the same continuity and interest in clients as the workers who currently determine welfare and Medicaid eligibility, since they do not know details of the case.

In Utah eligibility determination is still the function of the Department of Social Services, and enrollment is still the function of the Department of Health Services. Eligibility and enrollment personnel are, however, located in the same place so that eligible individuals can meet with or schedule an appointment with the enrollment representative after they have completed their assessment interview. Although the program is voluntary, over 90 percent of Medicaid beneficiaries have joined it because enrollment is tied to the actual date of eligibility determination or recertification and because enrollment officials are specifically trained in health care and health education.

In Kentucky the Department of Social Services is responsible for determining eligibility and for enrolling Medicaid beneficiaries, and both functions are performed by one person—the case worker. Individuals eligible for the program are mailed a notice that explains the necessity of enrolling in Citicare and of choosing a primary care physician, which they must do through their case worker. After the first notification, 40 percent of the individuals eligible for enrollment had selected a primary care physician.

In contrast to the other programs, the Santa Barbara Health Authority itself is responsible for conducting enrollment and has contracted this function to a fiscal agent, Jurgovan and Blair (JBI). Initially, a two-month lag occurred between eligibility determination and enrollment, causing problems in enrolling the Medicaid population. As a result some eligibles were not enrolled, and individuals no longer eligible were enrolled by mistake. Beneficiaries select their primary care provider through the mail, a procedure that had a 60 percent response rate. There has therefore been a 40 percent rate of assignment to physicians by computer. There seems to be a trade-off: it is more difficult to coordinate activities when two agencies are involved, but an outside agency can provide expertise otherwise lacking and thereby increase the probability of the program's success.

Program Administration

The experimental programs differ in some aspects from current Medicaid programs and, as a result, may require other methods of computer programming and administration. Since the staff of the Medicaid program often does not have the expertise needed for running these new programs, states must decide whether to administer their programs within the state government and, if so, whether to use existing staff or to appoint new staff or, if not, whether to contract with an outside agency. Not surprisingly, states have made different decisions based on their own experience and internal capability. The Michigan program is administered by existing staff in the Department of Social Services. The Utah program is administered within the Department of Health Care Financing of the Utah Health Department. Both programs began by introducing a case management system that reimburses physicians on a fee-for-service basis; they have initiated programs not radically different from their current Medicaid program. To a large extent, therefore, these states have felt confident to run the programs themselves. Since these demonstrations are implemented in only a few counties, they must be run in tandem with the traditional Medicaid program.

Santa Barbara and Kentucky, in contrast, have initiated programs that totally restructure care, centering it on a primary care "gate keeper" and capitation payment. A gatekeeper (often called case manager) is a primary care physician responsible for overseeing and providing for the health needs of the patient. A Medicaid beneficiary must have all of his or her care authorized by the gatekeeper. A capitation payment is a fixed dollar amount paid by the state to the health plan for each beneficiary. Plans are responsible for delivering all care for this capitation. Each of these programs is run by an independent agency under contract to the state. The reasons for choosing this structure include the greater administrative flexibility of an independent agency than of the state government; the ability to purchase sophisticated computer hardware and software necessary for processing claims, often precluded by statewide purchasing freezes; and the ability to monitor enrollment, processing of insurance claims, and the capitation rates, a function states have not previously undertaken. In addition, contracting the administration of health plans to an outside agency shifts much of the financial risk for a program from the state to the independent agency.

Programs also vary in the ways that provider groups (physicians, hospitals, laboratories, and pharmacies) are paid under the new Medicaid system as well as in the extent of financial risk these groups assume. Risk-sharing and remuneration systems have been developed to take into acount the reaction of providers. The most significant difference among the plans is in the way physicians are paid. Although all of the programs are designed around a primary care gatekeeper, in Michigan and Utah the primary care physicians and all specialists are paid on a fee-for-service basis. In Santa Barbara and Kentucky, the primary care physicians are paid on a capitation basis, but the nature and the extent of the capitation differ.

Programs differ in the way they reimburse specialists and hospitals. The Santa Barbara Health Initiative has negotiated all inclusive per diem hospital rates. Michigan retains cost-based reimbursement for its hospitals. Utah reimbursed hospitals on the basis of charges at the beginning of the program and has now adopted diagnosis-related groups. Citicare in Kentucky, however, has left arrangements for hospital care and the appropriate method of payment to the individual primary care physician or physician group. Although fee-for-service, charge-based reimbursement was the primary method of reimbursement at the beginning of Citicare, there are indications that this method will change and that individual groups will negotiate for discount rates or will collectively do so with the help of Citicare.

Although many primary care physicians are at risk, they range from being at full risk and sharing in profits and losses to being at partial risk and sharing only in profits, with losses made up through contributions to a risk pool funded jointly by the state and the physicians themselves. Furthermore, there are differences in what is included in the capitation payments for primary care physicians; some physicians are at risk for authorized specialty care and hospitalization, and others are not.

Utilization Review and Quality Assurance

Another concern of plans and states is the appropriate method of reviewing utilization and ensuring quality. Plans define quality assurance and utilization review, and design their monitoring methods differently. Even so, each program's system of utilization review is based on the Surveillance and Utilization Review System (SURS) routine, certified by the Health Care Financing Administration, which allows states to track physician utilization profiles and billing practices. In the two states that have maintained fee-for-service payment methods, paid claims still form the basis of the data in the SURS system. To do utilization review, SURS is simulated in Santa Barbara by the outside administrator's requiring that all primary care physicians submit pseudo-Medicaid bills. This simulation is enhanced because in Santa Barbara actual fee-for-service billings are debited to individual primary care physicians' accounts. Since primary care physicians are paid on a per capita basis, however, they do not have the incentive to submit pseudoclaims, and this can cause a problem for both utilization review and setting the capitation rates. Further explanation is included in the chapter on Santa Barbara.

Although overutilization is the major concern tackled by these demonstrations, underutilization is also a concern of all, especially critics. Utah and Kentucky, in fact, have also chosen to work cooperatively with the medical society to define standards of care so that underutilization might be identified. Even though procedures to identify it are in place, because underutilization is not easy to define, the success of these efforts is unclear. Despite good intentions these programs are almost never implemented on time, if at all.

The last issue concerning all sites is what incentives they should provide to encourage beneficiaries to join the plans. Even states with mandatory programs face a problem of getting beneficiaries to choose a case manager. They also face the risk that extensive enrollment and market penetration will actually increase costs if a substantial number of beneficiaries who currently do not use medical services join and have a capitation fee paid on their behalf. The HCFA has allowed, through its waiver process, the use of certain incentives: for example, guaranteed eligibility for up to six months or reductions or eliminations of copayments for services for the medically indigent. In this way, individuals who would otherwise lose their Medicaid benefits because of lack of eligibility could retain them if they chose the demonstration. The medically indigent would have fewer out-of-pocket costs if they were in the program.

This section has described some of the problems faced by all of the plans studied. More detailed information about each program follows in the individual case studies. The concluding chapter highlights some of the differences and similarities among the program structures and implementation processes.

2
The Michigan Physician
Primary Sponsor Plan

Michigan suffered disproportionately during the recent years of a troubled national economy. Heavily dependent on the auto and related industries, Wayne County, home of Detroit and the most densely populated county in the state, experienced pockets of unemployment as high as 25 percent. Despite an overall declining population, the eligible Medicaid population in Wayne County remained stable during the 1980–1983 period.

Soaring costs in the Medicaid program, due to rising medical care prices and increased use of outpatient facilities and emergency rooms, precipitated an unusual legislative challenge to the Michigan Department of Social Services (DSS), which administers the Medicaid program, and to the state's medical societies and hospital associations. The 1981 Appropriations Act included language that charged these state administrators and physicians with developing an alternative reimbursement system for physicians that would save at least $30 million. The state legislature also authorized over $6 million for incentive fees for providers who participated.

Several proposals were received. The one selected was a cooperative response in which the Michigan State Medical Society (MSMS) and the Michigan Association of Osteopathic Physicians and Surgeons (MAOPS) proposed a case management system. MSMS and MAOPS, together with the DSS, designed the Physician Primary Sponsor Plan (PPSP). The plan covers 280,000 Medicaid recipients in Wayne County. Implementation started in July 1982 and proceeded gradually over the course of a year; participation by recipients is mandatory. The great majority of the plan's enrollees qualify for Medicaid under Aid to Families with Dependent Children (AFDC) or disability insurance eligibility criteria. Medicaid recipients who are in a long-term care facility, are eligible for Medicare, are enrolled in a health maintenance organization, or are eligible for Medicaid under the medically needy program are excluded from participating in the plan.

Under the PPSP, each Medicaid recipient must choose a "primary sponsor" physician or an HMO for his medical care. The primary sponsors manage and coordinate all the care for the Medicaid beneficiaries enrolled with them. They provide primary care and arrange and authorize all other services, including referrals for specialty care, laboratory services, and hospital care (except for emergencies). The physicians receive the usual fee-for-service reimbursement plus a monthly case management fee of three dollars for each enrolled recipient.

The plan's purposes are to increase physicians' willingness to serve Medicaid recipients, to manage recipients' use of medical services better, to provide recipients better access to medical care, and to restrain Medicaid cost increases while paying physicians more reasonable fees. The case manager role played by the physician is critical to achieving these goals.

Operation of the PPSP

Physician Participation. Only about 60 percent of the 3,400 active physicians in Wayne County participated in the Medicaid program at the time the PPSP began. Although more than 90 percent of all physicians had participated five years earlier, the state had not raised the physicians' fee screens since 1977, and many doctors concluded that they lost money on each unit of service provided. The Medicaid program pays physicians about 60 percent of their charges, while it pays hospitals about 90 percent of their charges.

Compounding this unwillingness on the part of physicians to serve Medicaid clients is the fact that large areas of Detroit, usually the poorest sections, are underserved by physicians. As in most large cities, doctors are concentrated in the higher-income sections, leaving the poor to use local hospital clinics for their care.

State and medical society officials saw the Primary Sponsor Plan as a way to increase physicians' participation in the Medicaid program and to improve Medicaid recipients' access to medical care in their own communities. Many viewed the authorization of more than $6 million for case management fees as essentially a way to increase fees. In addition, many physicians had been reporting substantial decreases in patient activity because of the recession. A number were opposed to the increasing role of HMOs in the Medicaid program, which they viewed as interruptions of existing doctor-patient relations.

All providers offering primary care can become primary sponsors if they accept responsibility for managing all the medical care for their assigned Medicaid beneficiaries and agree to meet utilization and cost standards that were jointly developed by the DSS and the medical societies for use in monitoring the sponsor plan. The primary sponsor is directly responsible for providing primary care and for arranging and authorizing all other Medicaid-covered services, with the exceptions of vision, dental, and long-term care, mental health and life-threatening emergency services, which are considered automatic referrals. Furthermore, primary sponsors agree to provide twenty-four-hour coverage for their patients. This requirement has caused considerable concern among many independent practitioners who had not previously provided this extensive type of coverage. The requirement still stands, but physicians are allowed to make arrangements with other physicians for coverage with the understanding that any care rendered during this period shows up in the sponsor physician's utilization profile.

Several other issues arose early during the development of the sponsor plan. One issue concerned the participation of hospital-based physicians (those physicians who have their offices in organized outpatient departments in hospitals). Under the usual reimbursement method of the Medicaid program, these physicians receive a professional fee and the hospital receives an additional fee for the support staff, space, and overhead that it provides. The combined fees are typically much higher than the reimbursement obtained by physicians for similar services in their private offices. The medical societies strongly believed that all primary sponsors in the PPSP should be paid equally for equal work. The parity rule, as it came to be known, means that the hospital-based physicians receive the same fee as the community physicians and the hospitals do not get their overhead fees.

Hospitals were reluctant to participate in the PPSP because of the reduced reimbursement. Medicaid payments, however, constitute a substantial portion of their total revenues, and most Medicaid admissions come through the outpatient clinics. The Michigan Hospital Association proposed a compromise to the legislature that would allow physicians practicing on-site at hospitals to get the combined facility and professional fee while those practicing in hospital satellite clinics would receive only the professional fee. The proposal was part of the cost containment legislation that has twice been voted down by the legislature; as a result, the parity rule stands for now as the procedure in the PPSP.

Another issue, concerning the PPSP's limit of 1,500 recipients per primary sponsor, led to a lawsuit filed by a group of providers during the first month of the plan's implementation. The providers sued the state for potential damage to their medical practices. A temporary restraining order was put on the plan, and implementation halted.

The lawsuit claimed that the state had no demonstrable reasons on which to base a maximum of 1,500 patients per sponsor and that such a limitation would deprive some patients of access to care and would restrict the ability of some practitioners to generate income. Furthermore, the providers complained that due process had not been followed in promulgating the restriction on the number of recipients per sponsor. The court ruled in October 1982 that the limit on recipients per sponsor should be raised to 2,000 and that the plan should be gradually implemented to maintain doctor-patient relations for the time being. Moreover, if a physician had an established relationship with more than 2,000 beneficiaries, sponsorship under the PPSP could continue, but the case management fees would not be paid for those cases over the 2,000-patient threshold.

One result of the litigation was a delay in the implementation of the plan. By the end of 1982, however, 600 physicians had been approved as primary sponsors and had signed contracts with the state.

Incentives for Cost Containment. By making the primary physician responsible for the delivery of all medical care, and therefore presumably more cost conscious, the PPSP introduces an incentive to economize. The usual fee-for-service reimbursement method is preserved, and the monthly case management fee of three dollars per recipient is an additional inducement for physicians to participate.

Physicians who participate cannot suffer direct financial losses for failure to control the extent to which their patients use the system. The primary deterrent of "abusive" behavior by physicians is the threat of expulsion from the PPSP, which is accomplished through the use of physician profiles reflecting the use and costs of the specific services that the sponsors authorize for their enrollees each quarter. The data for laboratory tests, prescriptions, physical examinations, X-rays, specialty care, emergency room visits, and hospitalizations are adjusted for differences in age and sex of the patients under the care of each physician. Although the age and sex adjustment cannot erase case-mix differences, it adjusts for these factors to some extent and helps physicians who are routinely seeing sicker patients. The sponsoring physicians receive these periodic reports to help them monitor care more effectively.

Primary sponsors are evaluated in comparison with the other physicians in their specialty group (internal medicine, pediatrics, or family medicine). "Clean sponsors" are those who rank at or below the ninety-fifth percentile of costs or use in their peer group. "Provisional sponsors" are those who, over a three-month period, exceed the ninety-fifth percentile standard. The latter group's monthly case management fees are held in escrow while a DSS peer review committee decides if the care authorized by the physicians is appropriate. If the care is appropriate, physicians return to "clean sponsor" status and receive the escrowed case management fees with interest. If the care is deemed inappropriate, a physician has the option to ask for a court decision. A similar process is available under the traditional Medicaid peer review system. That experience has shown that cases take a long time to work through the courts and that, therefore, it is difficult to expel physicians from the program. In any case, this sanction is aimed only at outliers—those physicians whose practice patterns put them over the ninety-fifth percentile and cannot exert a major influence on the prevailing style of medical practice.

Beneficiary Enrollment. Enrollment of the 280,000 Medicaid recipients in the PPSP started in July 1982. The intention was to enroll them over the course of the following year at the rate of about 10,000 beneficiaries each month. Enrollment has lagged, however, and was only 38,000 by March 1984. The Medicaid recipients who used the health care system most extensively were the first enrolled during the phase-in peroid. The lack of computer capabilities prevented a speedier processing, since each enrollment selection had to be recorded by hand and sent in hard copy to the central computer to DSS in Lansing. Nine social workers were specially hired and placed in state offices for the telephone-based enrollment effort. Former case workers were hired because they were familiar with the welfare system and conversant with the problems of clients.

Initially the DSS sent each beneficiary a brochure briefly explaining the sponsor program and requesting the recipient to call in his choice of primary physician or HMO. Probably because it could easily be mistaken as advertising, the first mailing unfortunately generated a very poor response rate of only 18 percent. DSS sent beneficiaries who did not respond to the first letter a second letter advising them that they would be randomly assigned to a physician if they did not call in to choose a primary sponsor.

A high proportion of recipients did not call, and the social workers assigned them to participating physicians. Every fifth client was assigned to an HMO. Ideally beneficiaries should have been matched with doctors in their immediate neighborhoods or with physicians whom they had routinely been seeing. This information, however, was not available on the computer eligibility printouts that the social workers used to make assignments. As a result, recipients sometimes were assigned to physicians whom they knew but did not like, or to new physicians when they had already established primary care rela-

17

tions. This possibility also caused some physicians to fear that the plan was depriving them of their own patients. In addition, many patients had to travel long distances to their assigned doctors.

If beneficiaries requested a specific physician, they were enrolled with that physician as long as he or she had signed a contract with the state. When a beneficiary asked for a physician who had not signed with the state, the request was put in a "pending" category. This meant either that the physician was expected to sign on with the plan at a future date and the beneficiary would become an enrolled member at that time, or that the enrollment decision was postponed until a specified later date when more information about the requested physician's decision to participate in the PPSP was available. Social workers sometimes used this procedure deliberately to help clients stay out of the PPSP indefinitely. Clients were also allowed to change primary sponsors at any time with the proviso that the change would become active on the first day of the following month (if the request was made before the fifteenth of the month). Otherwise the wait would be six weeks.

Frequently recipients did not have established relations with primary care physicians and did not know whom to select when they did call in. This was particularly true of beneficiaries who had made little or no use of the medical care system. In these cases, the social workers tried to assess the needs of the patient and his family, such as requirements for language assistance, location, and specialty care. They then gave lists of physicians' names to the clients. The recipients could make their choices over the phone then or later.

Consumer Participation. Providers, through their two medical societies, were directly involved in the conception of the PPSP. The Division of Medical Assistance within the state's Department of Social Services administers the plan, but an appointed steering committee has assisted these state officials from the beginning. Membership on the committee includes the director of the Medical Services Administration, representatives of the two medical societies, two legislators, the director of the Department of Public Health, the governor's representative, a Medicaid client, and a representative from a public advocacy group. Hospitals are not specifically represented on the committee. The steering committee, which continues to meet on matters of policy, has also formed a smaller group that oversees the on-going implementation of the plan.

Because of pressure from consumer advocacy organizations, an additional consulting group, which included several Medicaid recipients and representatives from welfare rights organizations and public advocacy groups, later convened. The consumer advocates contended that recipients were not adequately represented in the planning process even though they were the ones most directly affected. Furthermore, the advocates were concerned that beneficiaries had little information to help them make decisions about which physicians would best meet their needs. Beneficiaries had no access to data on which physicians were most efficient and which physicians delivered the best quality of medical care.

These issues of the rights of beneficiaries led to a proposal by the consumer consulting group that it and the Division of Medical Assistance jointly draft a bill of rights. The group also requested that an ombudsman be appointed to represent recipients in any complaints. The Division of Medical Assistance rejected the idea of an ombudsman but agreed to help draft a bill of rights. The resulting document, "Rights and Responsibilities of the Beneficiary," focuses on recipient rights under the PPSP and on how beneficiaries can be responsible consumers. The document's effect on client behavior is unclear, however, because for lack of funds it was posted in physicians' offices but not sent directly to recipients. The consumer consulting group fears that the DSS has not properly distributed the bill of rights and that recipients do not see it.

The Michigan League for Human Services, under contract to the state, is conducting a nine-month study of the attitudes of consumers and providers toward the PPSP. Surveys will assess client satisfaction, providers' perceptions of the plan's weaknesses and strengths, and the ability of consumer advocacy groups to influence the plan's operation. The study will also investigate the nature of beneficiary complaints and overall administrative processes. In addition, the League for Human Services has a hot line that recipients can call if they need help with any aspect of the PPSP.

Other Reimbursement Initiatives. The Physician Primary Sponsor Plan is not the only attempt at an alternative reimbursement scheme to control Medicaid expenditures in Michigan. As early as 1978 the Department of Social Services instituted the Recipient Monitoring Project (RMP). Through a prior-authorization procedure the RMP tries to check the excessive use of Medicaid by a small number of beneficiaries. For recipients enrolled in the project, either a case worker or a specified primary care physician must authorize all medical care before it is rendered. The Recipient Monitoring Project continues to function today and has been successful in reducing the Medicaid use of its enrolled beneficiaries. The PPSP excludes all recipients who are part of the RMP in Wayne County.

For some time the state has been encouraging Medicaid beneficiaries to enroll with local health maintenance organizations. When the PPSP started, the Medicaid program had contracts with six HMOs, which enrolled over 75,000 recipients. The state estimates that it saves from 7 to 10 percent of the costs of providing care to enrollees because of cost efficiencies by the HMOs. Under the PPSP, if recipients are assigned to a provider, every fifth beneficiary is assigned to an HMO.

At the same time the PPSP was conceived, the steering committee that advises the Department of Social Services also designed a program called the Capitated Ambulatory Program (CAP), which does put primary care physicians at financial risk. Under the program, recipients may choose to obtain most of their primary care from a specific provider who is paid a fixed capitation to cover a negotiated package of medical benefits. The physicians are at risk for costs above the capitation rate, which cannot exceed 100 percent of projected charges under the traditional fee-for-service Medicaid program. The providers are also responsible for arranging and monitoring all services that they do not provide themselves. CAP is being implemented in Kalamazoo where the state has contracted with three group practices.

Implications for Cost Containment

The decision to implement the Physician Primary Sponsor Plan in Wayne County rather than in another, perhaps smaller, county was very controversial. On the one hand, Wayne County has the largest Medicaid population and the highest Medicaid program costs per capita. A successful program would therefore have the greatest savings potential there. On the other hand, because of the massive dimensions of the project, failure becomes a more likely possibility, and the visibility of Wayne County is high.

The state is planning to evaluate the PPSP and the other initiatives to determine how well they are meeting their objectives. The study will focus on differences in use by recipients among the PPSP, the Capitated Ambulatory Program, and a control group of Wayne County beneficiaries who are not yet entered in any special program. The evaluation will track use of specific services such as emergency room visits and hospitalizations. Severe methodological problems face the investigators. The effects of the PPSP or the alternative reimbursement programs are hard to sort out from the effects of other new regulatory measures and of the 1980–1983 recession. Moreover, unless the control group is representative of the PPSP's population, the findings will be biased. Until a report is released, analysis of the effects of the plan must rely on theory and speculation.

The following sections describe the potential effect of the PPSP on four of the Medicaid program's major problems: doctor shopping, emergency room use, "abusive" physicians, and excessive hospitalizations.

Potential Effect of the PPSP

Doctor Shopping. The propensity of some Medicaid recipients to visit numerous physicians for the same problem or set of problems has been labeled "doctor shopping." The reasons for this expensive behavior are not well understood. A number of theories have been advanced.

Because of the maldistribution of physicians through communities, "poor" quality providers—those with extremely high-volume clinics—tend to be located in areas most densely populated with Medicaid clients. Patients who are dissatisfied with the care they receive in such facilities may continue to look for alternative sources. Not knowing where to find higher-quality providers or how to use the health care system may make their search longer than necessary. Many providers probably appear inaccessible to these patients.

Another explanation concerns the life style of many recipients and the way in which they confront illness. Because of their economic circumstances, they may not be able to plan ahead by scheduling appointments. They deal with illness sporadically as crises arise and do not adhere to recommended follow-up care. Finally, some recipients doctor-shop because of drug addiction. They collect prescriptions from many doctors either to support their own habits or to generate income through sales of such prescriptions.

Because doctor shopping is most often caused by recipients' lack of access to adequate medical care, the PPSP should sharply reduce this unnecessary behavior. All patients in the plan must enroll with a specific primary care provider. While beneficiaries have considerable freedom of choice in selecting their physicians, some information, such as specialty, language, and location, is available to help them make their selections. For people who have never used the medical care system, the plan offers a designated entry point. And if recipients are dissatisfied with their assigned sponsor, the PPSP allows them to switch primary care physicians as frequently as they wish, as long as the necessary several-week administrative processing period is observed. This procedure allows beneficiaries to find the providers with whom they feel most comfortable.

Once beneficiaries are enrolled with primary care physicians, the sponsors function as gatekeepers and control all further referrals.

How diligent the sponsors actually will be in policing referrals probably is related to the degree of their financial risk. Except for expulsion from the program for extreme practice patterns (utilization higher than 95 percent of their peers), there are no incentives or risks for the participating physicians. The physicians receive the three-dollar case management fee, their behavior with regard to use and costs notwithstanding. If the providers could share in the cost savings produced through reduced doctor shopping, they would have more at stake in closely monitoring their referrals.

Another possible shortcoming concerns the way referrals are handled administratively. Specialists are required to submit their claims forms with the primary sponsors' Medicaid identification numbers on them as evidence that specialty care has been authorized. No written authorization is necessary; the specialist's office calls the primary sponsor at the time of service to obtain approval and the identification number.

Problems could arise if the telephone authorizations are difficult to obtain. Since specialists are likely to render care anyway and later ask the primary sponsors for retroactive approval, some specialists will assume blanket referral approval. The primary sponsors will have difficulty scrutinizing these specialists' claims. It is also possible that once sponsors' identification numbers are known, dishonest specialists will circumvent the system and submit claims without asking for approvals. Prior authorization via a referral form would be a preferred method.

Emergency Room Use. Emergency room care costs more than equivalent care given by physicians in their private practices. Medicaid recipients generally have high rates of emergency room use, and the reasons for these statistics are similar to those discussed for doctor shopping. Inadequate access to conveniently located private practitioners, the lack of information about how to find good physicians, and the sporadic, crisis-proportion medical needs of recipients all combine to make the emergency room the medical care site of choice for many beneficiaries. Moreover, emergency rooms are usually on main bus lines and are centrally located. They are convenient for Medicaid beneficiaries and safer too. Open twenty-four hours a day, they are usually protected by on-site security personnel. Private physicians serving the same neighborhoods are not open at night and cannot guarantee protection for their patients.

The automatic access to the medical care system, which is a by-product of the PPSP's assignment of beneficiaries to primary care practitioners, should reduce recipients' reliance on emergency rooms.

And if recipients do show up at a hospital's door with nonemergency problems, they are likely to be turned away once the hospitals understand the PPSP rules. Because of their institutional nature, emergency rooms are less likely than private specialists to give unauthorized care and to risk not being paid.

The primary sponsors must approve any emergency room visits that are not true emergencies. Because excessive use of high-cost emergency care would drive up the individual physician's cost profile, the gatekeeper has an incentive to eliminate unnecessary emergency room use. For the PPSP to be successful in controlling Medicaid program costs in this area, only the marginal physician need change his behavior.

The problem is in defining emergency care. Physicians are not accustomed to weighing the benefits and costs of each episode of care. They may find it difficult to evaluate the seriousness of patients' symptoms over the telephone. If the problem occurs during the day, patients will probably be encouraged to visit the physicians' offices. If the episodes happen at night, however, sponsors may not want to risk the possible medical and legal ramifications of incorrect decisions and may authorize care at the emergency rooms. If most sponsors behave this way, the entire group's use of emergency rooms will remain relatively high, and the likelihood of any individual physician's profile exceeding the ninety-fifth percentile will be correspondingly reduced. Since the PPSP can threaten to expel only such very high users, the effect of the sanction is lessened, and the plan may not have much effect on emergency room use.

Hospital-based physicians could be operating under a reverse incentive with regard to emergency room use. Hospitals receive full compensation for emergency room visits, but under the parity rule of the PPSP they may actually be losing money on each unit of service delivered in their outpatient clinics. A hospital's physicians, therefore, actually have an incentive to authorize care in the hospital's emergency room. As long as hospital-based physicians' cost and utilization profiles do not exceed the overall ninety-fifth percentile standard, the PPSP would not penalize such referral patterns.

"Abusive" Physicians. The Medicaid program regards as "abusive" those physicians who order far more office visits, tests, and procedures per patient than their colleagues. Although no exact guidelines define what constitutes abusive behavior, the Division of Medical Assistance has for some time established utilization norms through its peer review office, which is responsible for the Surveillance and Utilization Review System. Basically, abusive physicians are identified through their utilization profiles, which clearly distinguish them from their peers.

Differences in ordering and prescribing behavior can be explained, at least partially, by differing styles of care. A physician's style of care may predict which tests are ordered, their frequency, their sequencing, and their delivery on an inpatient or outpatient basis. It is well known that different regions of the country have varying styles of care as measured by rates of hospitalization and lengths of stay. As there are no widely established patterns of practice, it is not surprising that individuals' practices vary greatly. Physicians who are regarded as abusers argue simply that they provide the highest quality of care to their patients.

Economic theory can also explain the abusive behavior patterns of some physicians. Under the traditional Medicaid program design, physicians are financially rewarded for each service delivered. The more office visits and tests that the physician logs, the higher his income.

The PPSP has several deterrents to overuse. First, the plan will continue to operate the peer review system already in use in the Medicaid program. This system flags providers whose practice patterns are considered excessive and investigates their charges and services. Second, the use and cost profiles maintained on the primary sponsors will alert physicians to their standings in relation to their peers. The threat of being labeled a provisional sponsor by exceeding the ninety-fifth percentile standard and being excluded from participating in the plan is designed as the primary deterrent to overuse. Physicians who derive a large proportion of their income from Medicaid patients should be especially wary of the possibility of termination from the program.

Several procedural problems make it unlikely, however, that physicians who currently abuse the system will dramatically change their behavior. One problem is the lack of agreement by the professional community on what constitutes quality care. Any norms established by peer review panels might therefore appear arbitrary, and physicians can always argue that services are justified under the circumstances of their particular patients. Furthermore, physicians might question whether the use and cost profiles are adequately adjusted to reflect legitimate differences in case mix. The plan does adjust for age and sex, but if these variables are not well correlated with actual health status, physicians' practices might look systematically efficient or inefficient. There are no accepted measures for defining case mix in primary care practices.

Because any rule is easy to challenge, the judicial system will

24

likely arbitrate the issue of who is abusing the Medicaid program under the PPSP. The problem is that the judicial system provides so many checks and balances that the process is exceedingly slow. Physicians identified as provisional sponsors first appeal their classification to the peer review panel. If the panel decides the care rendered is inappropriate, the physician can bring a further appeal to an administrative court, which makes its findings on the evidence. Traditionally a notoriously long process under the Medicaid program, it is unlikely to be faster under the PPSP. Physicians will probably be retained in the program as provisional sponsors for at least a year before all appeals are completed.

The PPSP may have more effect on abusing specialists than on primary care physicians. The specialists have to rely on the primary sponsors to refer them patients. The potential effect of excessive specialist charges on the primary sponsor's profile will likely be sufficient to get the primary care practitioner to switch referrals from one specialist to another. If even a few primary care physicians take on this responsibility, the plan will save substantially for the Medicaid program.

Excessive Hospitalization. Hospitals take the largest share of the Medicaid acute care budget—over 30 percent—so the PPSP will ultimately be judged by whether it can reduce hospital admissions and lengths of stay. The more than fifty hospitals in Wayne County have much at stake, too. The new competitive environment has caused a number of hospitals to diversify their businesses and to market actively to private rather than to public patients. Many of them, however, still receive up to 30 percent of total revenues from the Medicaid program. And, unlike other locales, hospitals in Wayne County are unable to shift substantial costs from the public cost-based payers to commercial insurers because the charge-based payers compose only a small proportion of the market.

It will be difficult to differentiate the effect of the PPSP on hospital use from the effects of other programs and requirements already put in place by the state. No weekend elective admissions are allowed, for example, and the state requires second surgical opinions and prior authorization for certain surgical procedures. In addition, any beneficiary who stays in the hospital more than eighteen days must have prior approval, and any hospital case that exceeds the seventy-fifth percentile norm for use must have a review submitted to the state to receive payment.

The PPSP relies again on the gatekeeper concept and the threat of expulsion from the plan for excessive use as the main means for reducing hospitalization. Some physicians will certainly be more careful about whom they hospitalize because their cost and use profiles will provide them with new and better information than they had previously. Because hospital episodes are so costly, the primary sponsors have an interest in keeping patients out of the hospital or in minimizing their stays. Primary sponsors can reduce hospitalizations, for example, by doing diagnostic workups and laboratory work on an outpatient rather than an inpatient basis. In most cases, however, it is the specialist rather than the primary care physician who hospitalizes. The primary sponsors should encourage their referring specialists to change their styles of practice if admissions are too frequent. And if the specialists do not change, sponsors should switch their referrals to other doctors.

Cost savings from the PPSP through reduced hospital use will probably depend most on which doctors in the community participate in the plan. If the primary sponsors are affiliated with higher-cost hospitals, like teaching hospitals, then Medicaid's costs will remain high even if the physicians practice efficiently. Many of the physicians signed with the plan so far are hospital-based physicians affiliated with academic medical centers. While ideally sponsors should refer patients to lower-cost hospitals, most physicians will continue to admit patients to the hospital where they have admitting privileges and where they feel most comfortable. Because of this pattern of physician participation, the PPSP may not shift a significant proportion of Medicaid admissions from high-cost hospitals to low-cost hospitals.

Lessons Learned

The planned size of the PPSP program—enrollment of almost 300,000 beneficiaries over a twelve-month period—makes this one of the most ambitious case management programs yet implemented. There are several helpful lessons that come from implementing a large program within such a short period of time.

Not surprisingly, the acute health care cost crisis brought about by the recession of 1982–1983 made strong cooperation among the MSMS, the MAOPS, and the state feasible in a way that had not been possible before. When implementing change, it is probably never possible to satisfy all parties. Despite the sponsorship of MSMS and MAOPS, several physicians brought suit and lost. And several consumer groups were angered by the lack of consultation in the planning process. Nevertheless, a crisis can be the most propitious time for change.

By June 1984, eighteen months after implementation of the PPSP, the state of Michigan had not yet reached its enrollment goal of

280,000–300,000 beneficiaries; approximately 40,000 were enrolled. It is unrealistic to expect to implement a large program without the aid of a computerized, integrated eligibility and enrollment system. Eligibility is now determined through the standard process by the Department of Social Services. Computer printouts, often not up to date, are the basis of enrollment information; enrollment workers do not have on-line computer capacity. Eligibility status and enrollment matches cannot be easily checked since there is a manual, not an automated, filing system. Enrollment cannot be easily changed, and clients are frequently dissatisfied. The result has been fewer enrollees and potentially large forgone cost savings. Finding funds and taking care to develop appropriate software to support the eligibility determination, enrollment, and automatic assignment functions are critical to successful implementation. Such systems are also cost effective. Staff time can be minimized, space is saved because records can be stored on the computer, and cost savings can be enhanced by enrolling more individuals in the program. Whether the PPSP continues in the future is likely to depend critically on smoothing out such cumbersome "administrative" problems.

3
The Utah Choice of Health Care Program

By 1982 Utah, like most other states, had taken measures to control Medicaid costs by restricting program eligibility. Despite these efforts and the relatively low health care costs in Utah due to the youth and healthiness of its population, Medicaid costs continued to increase at an unacceptable rate. Medicaid expenditures exceeded $105 million in 1982, more than a 20 percent increase over 1981 expenditures.

Background of the Choice Program

The Utah Department of Health (DOH) sought new approaches to cost containment that would avoid further restrictions on eligibility under the program. The department wanted a system to guarantee access for beneficiaries to primary care physicians in a way that would also allow the state to be a prudent purchaser of care from doctors and hospitals. The Choice of Health Care program, which started operations in 1982, allows beneficiaries to choose between primary care physicians functioning as case managers and a federally qualified health maintenance organization. The case management system is voluntary for both recipients and physicians. Physicians who participate are required only to authorize or arrange all medical services for their enrollees. They are paid on a fee-for-service basis, and they are not placed at risk financially.

To understand the Choice program, we must review the political and regulatory environment in the state. Utah has been described as a state where the sovereignty of the family and the right to free enterprise are championed. Because of this background, the state legislature resisted implementing a certificate of need (CON) law in 1978, even though it was mandated by the federal government. Instead, the legislature authorized a study to determine whether a CON program is the best way to control hospital expenditures, or whether a market-oriented approach existed that would be more consistent with the philosophy of Utah's legislators.

The study, conducted by Lewin and Associates, drew two major conclusions. First, a CON law is necessary to control expenditures in the short run and should be authorized. Second, for the long run, the state should initiate a strategy to create competition among insurers with CON being phased out when the competitive system is in place and functioning. The competitive system should include the development of alternative delivery systems such as HMOs, independent practice associations (IPAs), and preferred provider organizations (PPOs).

The study also suggested that a private, nonprofit group be formed to stimulate interest in this competitive strategy among state and local governments and the business community. The Utah Health Cost Management Foundation was established as such an "all-payers" coalition. Its purpose is to address health care costs in Utah, and it has been active in sponsoring legislation to foster competition in health care.

At about the same time the study results became known, the state of Utah implemented a "lock-in" program for Medicaid recipients who were particularly high users of medical services. The lock-in program restricts freedom of choice of providers by the beneficiaries. They must go to designated primary care physicians. If their physician does not refer them, they cannot visit another doctor. After remaining in the system for a year, clients then return to the mainstream Medicaid program. State officials indicate that the program has successfully modified the use patterns of participating recipients, but data are still insufficient to show whether they will maintain their new health-seeking behavior patterns over time.

Because of the apparent success of the lock-in program, state officials determined that they could devise a similar program to address the problem of health care costs for the remainder of the Medicaid population. They also hoped to improve beneficiaries' access to care, since many recipients had no personal physicians, and to increase the participation of physicians in the Medicaid program. Only an estimated 50 to 60 percent of all physicians in Utah participated in Medicaid before the new program.

In late 1981 the Department of Health obtained a waiver from the federal government that allowed Utah to restrict beneficiaries' freedom of choice of provider. Shortly after that, department officials decided to implement a case management system with payments to physicians on a fee-for-service basis. They decided to proceed with a pilot program concurrent with efforts to build support among the health care provider and consumer communities. The pilot program started in March 1982 in Weber County and later in Salt Lake County.

The full program began operation in the summer of 1982 with almost no changes from the pilot. By July 1983 about 18,000 Medicaid recipients had chosen a case manager physician.

The Choice program aims at all Medicaid beneficiaries in the Wasatch front area (Salt Lake, Weber, and Utah counties). Seventy-five percent of Utah's Medicaid population of 55,000 live in the area covered by the program. Although all eligibility categories are included, recipients already enrolled in the existing lock-in program continue with it until their year is over.

Operation of the Choice Program

Physician Participation. Any physician licensed to practice medicine in Utah can serve as a case manager under the Choice program. A physician need not practice one of the traditional primary care specialties (internal medicine, family practice, pediatrics, or obstetrics) to qualify, but he or she must agree to function as a case manager as defined by the state. No special contract with the state is required as long as the physician is already a Medicaid provider. In addition, no maximum or minimum case loads have been established in the Choice program. Because there are no special contracts for the program, physicians may join or drop out as they wish. So far in the program, however, few physicians have disrupted continuity of care for patients by leaving the program.

The case managers coordinate all the care of the Medicaid beneficiaries enrolled with them. They must preauthorize all referrals for specialty care or hospital services on special referral forms. Specialists to whom recipients have been referred can order tests and prescriptions without the primary physician's authorization. The primary care physician, however, must be notified when a recipient is hospitalized and then must authorize referral care for the duration of the illness. The Department of Health is supposed to inform primary care physicians of all services provided by specialists on referral, enabling them to evaluate the specialists' behavior.

Beneficiaries must call their primary care physicians in emergencies to see if they can receive treatment in the physicians' offices; primary care physicians must be available or have someone cover for them on a twenty-four-hour basis. Other providers may give emergency treatment without authorization when a delay would pose a serious risk. Pharmacy, laboratory, and other ancillary services are controlled only indirectly since the primary care physician or the specialist must authorize their use.

Under the Choice program, patients are supposed to carry the referral forms to the specialists or hospital; specialists are responsible

30

for sending copies to the state. Theoretically, if a form is not filed with the state, the specialist will not be paid. Because the state's automated data processing system is not fully in place, however, the state has thus far been unable to track successfully the use of either primary care or referral services. Bills for unauthorized services, therefore, are frequently paid.

Incentives for Cost Containment. The Choice program compensates both primary care physicians and specialists on a fee-for-service basis. Utah chose this method even though it provides no financial incentive to control the use of physicians' services or of hospitals. Physicians operating within the program bill the state for services provided and receive payment according to a statewide fee schedule. The program selected the fee-for-service method of compensation both because it was practical and because it would attract physicians to the program.

First, the Utah Department of Health lacked the necessary expertise to establish a competitively based program with capitation rates. Except for the experience with the single HMO in Salt Lake City, no staff had worked with such programs. There was also a lack of data on the Medicaid population's utilization in previous years, making calculation of an appropriate capitation rate nearly impossible. Regardless of whether the rates are actuarially determined, negotiated with providers, or elicited through a bidding process, a prepayment program requires this kind of detailed data.

Second, and more important, was a general, communitywide suspicion of modes of payment other than fee-for-service. DOH officials thought that starting with the concept of gatekeeping and helping physicians become accustomed to caring for an enrolled population would be a first step toward a prepayment system. They believed that allowing physicians to continue to practice under the fee-for-service reimbursement method was the only way to attract doctors into the Medicaid program. No evidence yet suggests that physician participation in Medicaid has increased because of the Choice program.

Beneficiary Enrollment. A new Medicaid client's choice of health plan is made at the time that a Department of Social Services case worker determines eligibility for Medicaid. Beneficiaries already participating in the Medicaid program enroll at their regularly scheduled review sessions. Health plan representatives employed by the DOH handle the enrollment procedure. In the pilot program it was clear that social service workers perceived themselves as overworked and were insufficiently familiar with the health care system to provide adequate information to clients concerning their options. As a result DOH hired

31

nine health plan representatives with prior experience in health care or education and placed them in the social services offices where Medicaid eligibility is determined. These representatives are quite familiar with all the physicians in the community, and the cooperative arrangement between social services and health is running smoothly.

Clients choose between a federally qualified HMO with which the state has had a contract for seven years and the case management system. If the client chooses the case management system he then selects a primary care physician to serve as the case manager. Unlike some other states, Utah does not contract with the physicians to provide services. In Utah the patient has the responsibility for making the contact with the physician, thus ensuring that he will be enrolled with the provider with whom he feels most comfortable. Physicians also have the right to refuse recipients. The purpose of this approach is to encourage the development of stronger doctor-patient relations.

Frequently, however, patients do not know which physician to choose. When this is the case, the health plan representative tells them which physicians participate in the Choice program and their locations and specialties. The representative also supplies information on the HMO option. In addition, a videotape playing continuously in the social services waiting room describes the concepts of case management and HMOs. At the urging of the local welfare rights coalition, the DOH and the HMO jointly produced the videotape.

The selection of a primary care physician or an HMO commits the patient to that choice for a year. Beneficiaries who join the HMO may reconsider within thirty days, after which time they are committed to that choice for the next eleven months. If an individual who has chosen a case manager becomes ineligible for Medicaid and then regains eligibility later in the year, he remains committed to the same physician. Because Utah did not apply for a waiver from the federal government to guarantee eligibility for six months, it is likely that many beneficiaries will frequently go on and off the Medicaid, and therefore the Choice program's, rolls.

If a recipient does not select a physician at the time of eligibility determination, he will be called by a health plan representative and encouraged to return to choose a primary care provider. If he does not return, however, physicians are not automatically assigned. Although the Choice program is voluntary in this respect, about 92 percent of all eligible beneficiaries have chosen primary care providers or the HMO during the first year of operation of the program. The HMO has also increased its market share in Salt Lake City from less than 20 percent to more than 25 percent during this period.

Regulations permit the HMO to solicit enrollment by means of door-to-door canvassing conducted by its representatives. Potential enrollees learn of the HMO's services from these representatives and can, if they choose, select the HMO to provide their health care. Beneficiaries also complete a questionnaire to show that they comprehend the HMO's operation and restrictions. The HMO then retains the questionnaires to demonstrate that no marketing abuses have taken place. No evidence yet indicates whether this enrollment process, which is more accessible to the beneficiaries, has given the HMO an advantage over the case management alternative.

The HMO and the case management program send paper copies of all enrollment records to Salt Lake City for data processing and storage in a central computer facility. The state notifies participating physicians each month how many new beneficiaries have enrolled with them, but the names of the beneficiaries are not provided. Patients must then contact their case managers. Participating physicians are concerned about this system because they are always uncertain whether they are delivering care to patients legitimately enrolled with them.

The primary care physician or the HMO selected should also appear on a beneficiary's Medicaid card. The card identifies the patient to the primary care physician and alerts other providers not to treat him without prior authorization. Although the system should operate so that each month's Medicaid card will contain this information, inadequacies in the state's medical information system have not made this possible yet. Efforts are under way to improve the ability of the state's computer to provide up-to-date information. Without this it will be increasingly difficult to ensure that only legitimate care is reimbursed.

Consumer and Provider Support. During the implementation of the pilot program, the state representatives made extensive contacts with several interest groups concerning the Choice program and the concept of case management. While neither Utah Issues, a welfare rights group, nor the Utah State Medical Society had a formal role in the planning process, the help and ideas of both groups were sought. Initially both the consumer and provider groups expressed support. Utah Issues suggested an educational initiative, which resulted in the videotape previously discussed. The medical society helped to inform physicians of the program.

Utah Issues liked linking the beneficiary to the primary care provider because this arrangement would enhance access to care. The group was also enthusiastic about promises by the state for consumer health education. Enthusiasm dwindled, however, when the state legislature mandated that a system of copayments be instituted in Medicaid. These provisions would require Medicaid recipients to make copayments for certain services. Providers would be responsible for collecting them. Utah Issues believes copayments would impede access to care—an attitude purportedly addressed by the Choice program. After substantial protest by the affected groups, the copayment program was cut back significantly to apply only to unnecessary emergency room visits.

As the Choice program was implemented, the medical society also withdrew its support because of other developments with alternative delivery systems. In particular, a hospital chain attempted to start its own exclusive provider organization. The medical society objected to the planned inclusion of some physicians and not others. Fearing that the state might set similar limitations on the primary care network in the future, the medical society withdrew its support. It is currently considering starting its own independent practice association.

Other Reimbursement Initiatives. Although the case management system used by the Choice program is designed to influence and control the use of physicians' services, it does not affect the use of hospital services in a major way. Utah officials wanted additional measures to bring the problem of hospital costs under control, and they considered several approaches.

One option was a statewide or regional per diem system similar to the reimbursement method used for nursing homes in Utah. The state moved to a statewide, flat per diem rate reimbursement system for nursing home care in 1981. Under the two-tiered system, all skilled nursing facilities are paid the same per diem rate, and all intermediate care facilities are paid a different daily rate. So far the state has saved money with this system, and nursing home administrators have expressed satisfaction with it. The state did not adopt this approach for the hospital sector, however, because it would have had to develop multiple rates for the varying needs of different kinds of institutions.

Utah also considered implementing a hospital contracting system whereby the state would negotiate with hospitals and would award contracts to some of them, thereby preventing the others who did not get contracts from being reimbursed for serving Medicaid patients. A similar system has proven controversial in California where it has been reported to have led to financial problems for some hospitals that had depended heavily on Medicaid revenues but had not won contracts. Hospital administrators in Utah were hesitant to try this system.

Instead, Utah officials worked with hospitals and implemented a DRG-based (diagnostic-related groups) prospective payment system for hospitals on July 1, 1983, one year after the case management system was begun. Hospital administrators favored the DRG approach because they believed that their institutions delivered care efficiently and that there would be financial benefits under the system. Utah has the youngest and healthiest population of any state, and its hospital admission and length of stay rates are relatively low compared with other areas. Furthermore, because Medicaid payments compose only about 3 to 4 percent of total revenues in most Utah hospitals, there are opportunities to shift costs to charge-paying customers, as commercial insurance plans do, if the DRG-based payment system proves fiscally disadvantageous.

The combination of a case management system and a DRG-based hospital reimbursement system on such a broad scale is unique to Utah, except for a newly initiated plan in New Jersey. The state is using the same categories of DRGs being used to pay hospitals under the Medicare program. Utah, however, is using its own data to determine rates for each DRG category. A correctly designed DRG system should check hospital cost increases that would otherwise result from unnecessarily long stays. But neither the case management system nor the DRG approach may have much effect on the number of admissions to hospitals. Because physicians take no financial risks under the fee-for-service payment system, some officials are skeptical that these physicians will perform the gatekeeping function adequately.

Implications for Cost Containment

The goals of the Choice of Health Care project for the Medicaid program are to control the excessive use of health care services, to improve access to care for beneficiaries, and to increase physician participation. Like the primary care networks in other states, the Choice program enrolls beneficiaries directly with primary care physicians. This link alone should improve recipients' access to care and eliminate much unnecessary use of health services, such as unwarranted emergency room visits.

The Choice program, however, offers physicians no deterrents to excessive use of medical services or incentives for the efficient practice of medicine. Under the fee-for-service reimbursement system, the physician shares no risks. Although the case manager is supposed to be the gatekeeper to the rest of the medical care system, under the Choice program primary care physicians can give referrals to specialists without even making a clinical assessment. Referral forms do not restrict the frequency or duration of visits to the specialist or hospital;

referrals are open-ended. More important, the case manager does not lose or gain financially, regardless of the number of visits or the costs of medical services.

Unlike Michigan's program, which is similarly based on fee-for-service payment, physicians in the Choice program are not paid a case management fee (a monthly payment for services as a case manager); the provider has no financial incentive to participate as a case manager. Recently fees for physicians' services under Medicaid were increased in Utah. If fees are not raised or are even cut in the future, many physicians may drop out of the program.

Lessons Learned

Despite these shortcomings, the Choice program teaches several important lessons. First, the Department of Health chose to implement a system that was acceptable to providers and consumers, and it attempted to maximize support from both groups. The DOH informed consumers about the program during its earliest stages and solicited their suggestions. The state asked the local medical society to sponsor the pilot programs jointly. The physician group eventually gave its support because the program retained the fee-for-service payment system. These efforts to work with interest groups enhanced the successful implementation of the program.

Second, the case management program, though ultimately operated in a large, densely populated area, was implemented slowly so that problems could be detected and dealt with before the entire program was affected. Two voluntary pilot programs were conducted by the state during the spring of 1982. During the pilot programs, physicians became accustomed to the concept of referral forms and did not later find the increased paper work overwhelming. Recipients had time to learn about the case management system and HMOs in their social service offices. When the full-scale implementation began in the summer of 1982, no delays occurred.

Careful planning by the Department of Health smoothed the implementation of the Choice program. There have been no lawsuits and no loud grievances from either recipients or physicians. Whether this incremental approach will ultimately make a prepaid capitation system more acceptable to physicians remains to be seen. The long-term success of the case management program probably depends on the ability of the state to move to such a prepayment system.

4

The Kentucky Citicare Program

Kentucky's Medicaid spending rose over 700 percent from 1971 to 1983. The decline in the proportion of dollars paid by the federal government further exacerbated the budgetary effect of this huge increase. Whereas at the inception of the Medicaid program the federal share by formula was 80 percent, by 1982 the federal share had dropped to 68 percent. Remarkably, the eligible population remained relatively stable throughout this period, even as costs soared. About 320,000 people, or 9 percent of Kentucky's population, are eligible for benefits under the Medicaid program at any given time. The cost increases, therefore, result from higher prices for medical services and expanded use of those services, rather than from the use of services by more people.

Development of Citicare

Faced with a predicted funding shortfall, the Kentucky legislature during its 1980 session devised a number of cost containment measures for the Medicaid program. These reforms included a prospective reimbursement system for hospitals, reduced reimbursement for physicians' services in hospitals, mandatory second opinions for elective surgeries, preauthorizations for all hospital admissions, required preadmission laboratory testing, and reduced allowable hospital days. A second set of changes, implemented in conjunction with adjustments made by the Budget Reconciliation Act of 1981, resulted in dropping 33,000 AFDC eligibles from the Medicaid rolls.

At the same time that these cost containment programs were being implemented in 1981, the University Hospital in Louisville, the primary teaching hospital of the University of Louisville Medical Center, suffered a severe budget deficit and requested a $2 million bailout from the state secretary for human resources. The University Hospital traditionally supplies most care for the indigent of Jefferson County, which includes Louisville. Without the financial reprieve, the hospital claimed it would be forced to turn away Medicaid patients. In response, the state granted the needed funds with the proviso that the

Medicaid health care delivery system be restructured so that such financial crises would not arise in the future.

A Medicaid task force was appointed with representatives from the state, county, city, and county board of health. At the end of 1981, the task force recommended a new initiative it named Citicare. Citicare, which began operations in the summer of 1983, is a prepaid primary care network serving Medicaid beneficiaries in Jefferson County, where about 25 percent of the total eligible population in Kentucky lives. Each recipient selects a primary care provider (physician, clinic, or HMO), with changes permitted after a year. Participating physicians provide primary care services, including internal medicine, family practice, pediatrics, and obstetrics, for their clients and arrange for all other covered specialty and hospital services. In return, providers are paid a monthly capitation fee for each enrolled beneficiary that covers primary care and referral physician services, and home health care. Primary care physicians bear the financial risk for these services if use is higher than anticipated. Citicare also incorporates fiscal incentives to reduce overutilization of hospital services.

As originally proposed, Citicare was to serve both those categorically eligible for Medicaid and those eligible under the medically needy program of Jefferson County. The medically needy group consists of those who are ineligible for Medicaid but still qualify for medical aid under the income-level rules established by city and county assistance programs. The Medicaid task force had calculated that if the total expenditures by the city, county, and state for all medically indigent persons were pooled, there would be sufficient funds to care for all recipients under Citicare without further reductions in eligibility or coverage. Louisville and Jefferson County officials, however, refused to combine their funds with state and federal dollars because they wanted to remain autonomous and to divest themselves entirely of the indigent care problem. Because of these funding limitations, the Citicare program now covers only AFDC and AFDC-related beneficiaries. The 40,000 AFDC recipients make up about 80 percent of the Medicaid clients in Jefferson County. Although this younger population of primarily mothers and children constitutes a healthier initial group for which stable and accurate predictions of costs can be made, the Citicare concept is expected to be extended eventually to other segments of the indigent population as well as to Medicare and private sector groups.

Operation of Citicare

Administration. Citicare, Inc., an independent, not-for-profit corporation, and not the state of Kentucky, is responsible for implementing and operating the Citicare program. It is responsible for delivering to the AFDC beneficiaries a comprehensive health benefit package, including physicians' services, emergency care, hospitalization, home health care, health assistance, ancillary services, and drugs. Other benefits covered by the Medicaid program, but not provided by Citicare, are available to AFDC beneficiaries under the traditional fee-for-service system.

For several reasons, a nongovernmental organization was formed to operate Citicare. There were concerns, for example, that the state government did not have the appropriate experience to negotiate physician contracts and to design information and quality-assurance programs. Although primary care networks were a relatively new concept for everyone, it was also believed that consumers were less likely to sue an independent body than they were the state, if they protested the lack of freedom in their choice of physicians. Furthermore, a private organization seemed to have more flexibility than the state in negotiating with physician groups.

The Health America Corporation (formerly Health Plans, Inc.) of Nashville, Tennessee, won the contract from Citicare, Inc., to administer the Citicare program. Health America, which manages HMOs throughout the country (the best known being the Group Health Plan of Northeast Ohio), has had much experience delivering care to the indigent population. Many of the utilization review and accounting systems to be used in Citicare were adapted from other successful plans operated by Health America.

Health America reports to the board of directors of Citicare, Inc., which includes representatives from the city board of health, the state Cabinet for Human Resources, and various provider groups. The board makes policy decisions and must approve the candidates recruited by Health America for executive director and medical director. The first director of Citicare is a highly respected family physician who is a native of Louisville, has practiced in the community for more than thirty years, and is a founder and past president of the Academy of Family Physicians.

Initially the state planned to qualify Citicare as an HMO so that it could obtain a waiver from the federal government, allowing Medicaid beneficiaries to be locked in with selected providers. The Waxman amendment to the Tax Equity and Fiscal Responsibility Act's sections on Medicare and Medicaid HMOs, which passed Congress in the fall of 1982, changed the rules for HMOs and Medicaid recipients. It prohibits states from forming a primary care network that does not contract for care with a federally qualified HMO. It preserves the right of recipients to choose their providers, and precludes non-HMO providers such as physicians in solo practice from accepting financial risk for hospitalizations and all other care, to avoid creating incentives for withholding necessary care.

Instead Citicare, Inc., is qualified as a health-insuring organization (HIO). An HIO contracts for medical services provided to beneficiaries in return for premiums or subscription fees. Unlike an HMO, it may not deliver services itself. There is no guaranteed eligibility period for AFDC recipients under the program, nor are there requirements that the HIO must be composed of no more than 75 percent Medicaid enrollees. Also unlike an HMO, the HIO has no federal requirements for covered health benefits, but it must assume an underwriting risk. Therefore, Citicare, Inc., is at risk for 2 percent of total capitation payments under the program. The Health America Corporation assumes this risk through a bank line of credit. Health America receives an additional 5.8 percent of total capitation funds (for a total of 7.8 percent) to administer the program. The state government has worked successfully with Health America thus far in implementing the Citicare program. Some critics argue that the Cabinet for Human Resources might have been able to administer the program more cheaply itself, but there are no data to substantiate this claim.

Physician Participation. All primary care physicians in Jefferson County may elect to participate in the Citicare program. They must be willing to provide prepaid primary care services to AFDC beneficiaries, and they cannot turn away any enrolled recipient. To minimize the probability of adverse selection, physicians must agree to accept a minimum of 300 enrolled patients. The maximum number of recipients who can enroll with a single doctor is 1,800 patients. Finally, participating physicians must be willing to provide twenty-four-hour coverage for their practices, which means, in effect, that they must make arrangements with colleagues for covering their practices when they are unable to take their own calls.

When the Citicare program started in July 1983, about 300 of the 750 practicing primary care physicians in Louisville joined. Their specialties included family practice, internal medicine, pediatrics, and obstetrics/gynecology. While the majority of these individuals already served Medicaid patients, participation increased from 29 to 40 percent. The reasons for the relatively low participation by physicians are probably not unique to Louisville. Historically, even under conditions of limited risk, physicians have been unwilling to treat Medicaid patients because of the extensive paper work required for billing claims and because of the low levels of payment. When physicians are also asked to share in the risk of cost overruns, it is not surprising that they would often hesitate, even when certain offsetting incentives are provided. Nevertheless, the administrators of Citicare believe this is more than enough physicians to begin the program.

In fact, Citicare has not been able to enforce the minimum of 300 patients. Since there are only 40,000 enrollees and 300 physicians, there are not enough enrollees to go around. Primary care physicians are not at risk for losses during the first year of the program. Thus primary care physicians with fewer than 300 enrollees have been permitted to participate. In the second year, when primary care physicians are to assume risk, the plan will be to offer these physicians the opportunity to renew their contracts with the warning that renewal may be financially unsound. Physicians may also drop out of Citicare.

Physicians have also expressed specific concerns about Citicare through the county medical society. Although the Jefferson County Medical Society originally endorsed the plan and now, because of a change in leadership, officially neither endorses nor opposes it, individual members think the program causes breaches in the doctor-patient relation and reduces the quality of medical care. These doctors fear that patients might distrust their physicians' recommendations for therapies, procedures, or hospitalization if the providers stand to gain or lose financially based on whether patients follow these recommendations. Such distrust could reduce compliance by patients and, consequently, lower the quality of care. Moreover, these physicians believe that the primary care providers in Citicare are implicitly required to deliver a broader range of services than they were trained to provide. Because there is a financial incentive to minimize referrals to specialists, primary care physicians might attempt to perform common procedures, such as pelvic examinations or allergy testing, that they would not otherwise provide. Critics of Citicare think this tendency might result in reduced quality of care for the Medicaid patients. Proponents, however, view such procedures as within the mainstream of primary care. They claim physicians who are unwilling to treat such cases themselves are not really primary care physicians.

Some physicians admit they simply do not like the concept of prepayment. They would prefer a case management system that retains fee-for-service payments or an independent practice association (an IPA is a model of an HMO that allows physicians to remain in their offices and collect on a fee-for-service basis). The Jefferson County Medical Society is investigating the feasibility of starting an IPA, but such a development is at least several years away.

More than 180 of the 300 physicians who have signed with Citicare are associated with the University of Louisville Medical Center, and the great majority of these doctors are residents in the family practice and pediatrics programs. These are the physicians who have traditionally served the AFDC population in Louisville.

The physicians at University Hospital are reorganizing to meet the challenges of the Citicare program. Outpatient care at the hospital is expensive compared with similar care provided in a private physician's office. Medicaid now pays the hospital an average of $37 per visit for overhead and support expenses in addition to the physician's fee. To cut costs, the Department of Pediatrics has opened two new clinics away from University Hospital. One is near the hospital, and the other is located in an underserved area of southwest Louisville. The pediatricians hope to strengthen their image in the community and, at the same time, build their teaching programs in pediatrics and family practice. To avoid alienating private physicians in the community, the pediatricians obtained the county medical society's endorsement before starting the clinics.

Despite an active marketing program that included posters, radio advertisements, and billboards, enrollment with the university pediatricians has not met expectations. The clinics need 5,000 patients to break even, but only 4,000 Medicaid recipients selected them during the initial Citicare enrollment period. One reason for the low enrollment might be that although many recipients use the University Hospital clinics sporadically, they may not consider the university physicians as their personal doctors or their usual sources of care. Another factor might be the perception that the university's Citicare clinics are located at University Hospital, which is inconvenient for most Medicaid beneficiaries.

The Humana Corporation, which manages the University Hospital, has also committed itself to building three "access" clinics to serve indigent patients of all ages. When the Humana Corporation won the state contract to manage University Hospital in 1983, it agreed to build the clinics to ensure access and continuing care for the poor. One clinic has been opened west of downtown in an area densely populated by AFDC beneficiaries. Staffed by university physicians, it will participate in the Citicare program.

Several other large provider groups participate in the Citicare program. Two community health centers on the west side of Jefferson County, originally started with funds from the Office of Economic Opportunity, have welcomed Citicare as a new opportunity to offer improved service to their existing patient population. Louisville's only federally qualified HMO, Health Care of Louisville, is also participating in Citicare. It is owned by Health America Corporation, the same organization that manages Citicare. The HMO has recently grown rapidly to a total enrollment of 18,000 in Louisville. It currently treats about 1,000 Medicaid patients under a direct contract with the U.S. Department of Health and Human Services, and it has agreed to accept an additional 1,000 patients under the Citicare program. Although Health Care of Louisville is willing to discuss expanding the enrollment in the future, at present it cannot accept additional Citicare patients because of capacity limitations.

Incentives for Cost Containment. Citicare receives from the state a monthly capitation payment of $46.55 for each recipient. Of this amount, 0.2 percent is retained by Citicare for incidental expenses, such as board meetings. The remaining 99.8 percent has been budgeted to the following accounts: the physicians capitation (26.3 percent), the hospital management reserve (53.6 percent), Health America (7.8 percent), the obstetrics pool (3.9 percent), drugs (3.0 percent), laboratory services (1.4 percent), out-of-area services (0.4 percent), health education (0.2 percent), and others (3.4 percent). The allocations are somewhat arbitrary and were based on previous Medicaid expenditure patterns.

The primary care providers who participate in the Citicare program receive a monthly capitation fee for each patient enrolled with them. The fee is adjusted for three age categories (birth to two, $25; two to twenty-one, $11; and over twenty-one, $13), but because the program covers only AFDC recipients, no other adjustments are necessary for eligibility. By accepting the capitation payment, the physicians assume financial responsibility for delivering and coordinating their patients' care.

Twenty-six percent of all the revenue that Citicare, Inc., receives from the Medicaid program is allocated for physician capitation payments. The physicians' capitation is divided into three parts. Fifty percent is paid directly to the primary care physicians each month for their services. Thirty percent is placed in a fund called the "allocation for referral services" and used to pay for referral specialty services, professional services provided in emergency rooms, and home health care services. Consulting specialists are paid on a negotiated fee schedule similar to the one already in use by Medicaid. When a service is rendered for which there is no existing Medicaid fee, a fee is derived from Blue Shield data. The remaining 20 percent of the physician capitation payment is retained as a "hospital withhold" to make up any deficits incurred in the allocation for referral services and to cover hospitalization expenses beyond the amount allocated in the hospital management reserve.

In the first year of operation the primary care physician can lose up to the entire 20 percent hospital withhold plus 15 percent of the allocation for referral services if expenses for medical services run very high. The physician is not liable, however, for any expenditures that exceed the aggregate physician capitation payment; a reinsurance fund held by Citicare, Inc., would pay such expenses. In subsequent years of operation, however, the physicians will be at risk for 5 percent of any expenditures that exceed the total capitation amount allocated to them. To cushion the physician's liability from catastrophic illness, each provider's financial risk is capped at $5,000 per episode of illness.

Citicare incorporates significant financial incentives for participating physicians to practice efficiently. If a primary care physician's authorized referrals are less than actuarially predicted, he receives the balance retained in the allocation for referral services at the end of the year. Likewise, any surplus in the hospital withholding fund is distributed to all primary care physicians who maintain positive balances in their capitation accounts. The total amount of possible rebate to an individual physician is limited to $10,000. Surpluses are distributed to physicians in proportion to the number of patients enrolled. Physicians who have negative balances in the allocation for referral services and the hospital withhold, however, simply forfeit the amount of the withhold.

A separate hospital management reserve, consisting of approximately 54 percent of Citicare's total funds, is maintained to cover inpatient hospital services and certain outpatient services not included in the physicians' capitation (X-rays and institutional charges for emergency room services). Hospital charges are paid at prevailing Medicaid per diem rates unless Citicare, Inc., or the participating physicians can negotiate other arrangements with individual hospitals. Any surplus in this hospital reserve fund at the end of the year is evenly divided between participating physicians who have positive balances in their capitation accounts and Citicare. If there are any aggregate cost savings at the end of the year, $250,000 is set aside for unanticipated catastrophic expenses, such as individual episodes of illness that exceed $5,000; the state of Kentucky receives two-thirds of any remaining funds and Citicare one-third.

Citicare, Inc., contracts with the International Clinical Labs (ICL) for laboratory services. ICL was selected through a competitive bidding process. Citicare, Inc., issued a request for proposal asking for bids on the twenty most common laboratory tests. Seven firms expressed interest, and three ultimately submitted responses to the request. ICL was the lowest bidder. Citicare pays ICL a fixed amount per test, which they estimate to be 50 percent of the ICL list price. ICL has four stations throughout greater Louisville to which tests may be taken. ICL also guarantees daily pickup at physicians' offices and twenty-four-hour turnaround time.

Physicians who have their own laboratory facilities may not use them under Citicare; this has produced great concern. Citicare will, however, pay any licensed laboratory used by physicians its charges or the ICL fee, whichever is less. Pharmacists receive payment under the current reimbursement methods of the Medicaid program—maximum allowable cost per prescription plus a small dispensing fee. Citicare has contracts with all chain pharmacies in the Louisville area. Originally Citicare proposed buying pharmacy services on a capitation basis, but pharmacists feared capitation would cut their profits even more than the low dispensing fee that Medicaid already paid. Physicians are not at financial risk for the use of either drugs or laboratory tests under Citicare.

Citicare is also developing a special incentive plan called the Home Assistance Program (HAP) to limit expenditures for hospital care. Under HAP, patients who leave the hospital early with the permission of their primary care physician can collect up to $50 per day to purchase special assistance that would enable them to recuperate at home. The physician has an incentive to release patients early to minimize risk to the hospital withhold fund, and patients appreciate getting home earlier. It is possible, however, that beneficiaries may view the per diem vouchers as a means to obtain extra income rather than as a substitution of home care for hospital care. It will be necessary to monitor for potential abuse in the program. HAP is funded from the hospital management reserve.

Beneficiary Enrollment. Although Health America has responsibility for administering Citicare and handling enrollment problems after an individual has first joined, the state Cabinet of Human Resources is responsible for enrolling beneficiaries with primary care physicians. Enrollment of the 40,000 AFDC beneficiaries took place in social services offices in three waves. At the time the project was initiated, only about 50 percent of the Medicaid recipients in Jefferson County already had a personal physician.

During the summer and fall of 1982, beneficiaries could join the Citicare program voluntarily. Providers continued to be paid on a fee-for-service basis during this voluntary period to give them and recipients an opportunity to acquaint themselves with the program before full implementation.

The great majority of recipients enrolled during May and June of 1983. The Citicare program began on July 1 for those who enrolled in

May and on August 1 for those who enrolled in June. Beneficiaries had to select their primary physicians in person during appointments with their social workers. In certain circumstances a relative was permitted to make the selection, but a beneficiary could not enroll by telephone. Each beneficiary received an official letter notifying him of his appointment with a social worker. A glossy brochure explaining the program accompanied the letter from the state so that recipients would not mistake it for junk mail.

Despite this notification process and the publicity (frequently adverse) that surrounded the proposed Citicare project during the gubernatorial primary campaign in the spring of 1983, only 40 percent of all recipients appeared for their appointments with the social workers. Thus no mechanism for explaining to beneficiaries that participation in the program is mandatory appears to have been effective. Some argue that consumer group representation in the planning process would have increased beneficiary enrollment. While the more active involvement of such groups would certainly have enhanced communications, the community sessions held to explain and discuss the Citicare program were poorly attended. Moreover, other states that have involved consumer groups have experienced similarly disappointing results for voluntary enrollment.

Medicaid beneficiaries who attended their sessions with the social workers received a list of all physicians participating in Citicare with their specialties and office locations. More information was not given to the recipients because the state did not want to influence the selection process unduly. Recipients had to choose a physician from the list even if they had an established relation with a physician who was not participating in Citicare.

Citicare randomly assigned the 60 percent of the recipients who did not respond to the notification letter to participating providers and reviewed each beneficiary's claims history first to determine whether a participating physician had seen the patient during the past year. If so, Citicare assigned the recipient to that physician's panel unless the physician's quota had already been filled. When no usual source of care could be identified, matches were based on zip code. In the southwest section of Louisville, where many recipients lived but no physicians in private practice had signed with Citicare, patients were distributed among all participating physicians regardless of location.

The assignment mechanism has generated a predictable set of implementation problems. Recipients were often assigned to physicians who were on the other side of the city or practiced an inappropriate specialty. More troubling, recipients who enrolled in Citicare and were then removed from the rolls because of loss of eligibility were frequently assigned to a different physician when they again became eligible. These problems were resolved in the first three months of the program, however. The state replaced the computer assignment system with one in which a recipient's social worker manually assigned the client to an appropriate primary care physician. Occasionally computer mistakes are still made, especially ones that indicate an incorrect match between recipient and primary care physician.

It is impossible to know how many recipients were displaced from their usual primary care physician since so many were randomly assigned. Initially Citicare planned that after the first choice or assignment, each beneficiary would have the opportunity to change primary physicians during the first month. Later changes could be made only by appealing directly to the Citicare board of directors. Many beneficiaries, however, do not understand that they are locked into a single primary care provider until they actually seek care. Because Citicare believes that doctor-patient rapport is crucial if the program is to work, it has changed its plan and freely allows enrollees to switch their primary care physician. Primary care providers may also request that a patient be assigned to a new physician. Citicare checks, however, to make sure that a physician's request is related to lack of rapport with the patient and not to the patient's poor health. Similarly nonparticipating physicians are not well informed about the Citicare program. Thus the early months of the program were plagued with many requests for retroactive approvals of rendered care.

Claims Payment. In its contract with Citicare, Health America is responsible for payment of capitation to primary care physicians, fee-for-service claims payments to specialists and hospitals, financial accounting and development, and operation of a management information system (MIS). Health America uses data from its MIS to prepare for the state reports required by its contract. It also prepares reports for physicians of their utilization experience and the financial status of their risk pools.

Although Citicare capitation payments to primary care physicians have always been up to date, fee-for-service payments lagged behind substantially for the first three months, much to the distress of hospitals and specialists. During this period the volume of claims was large, and checks had to be written manually because an automated check payment system came into operation three to four months late.

Moreover, the MIS did not become fully operational until January 1984, and it was not until March that the first reports became available. More lead time seems to be needed to develop computer software.

Consumer Participation. Consumer advocacy groups, such as the Citicare Action Committee (a welfare rights organization) and the local legal aid organization, have complained that consumers were not included in the planning process for the Citicare program and that limited information about the program has been available from the state. Medicaid recipients, in fact, were not represented on the original task force that recommended the prepayment initiative, nor have beneficiaries helped in the development of instructional and educational materials about Citicare. Consumer groups believe that beneficiaries would be less skeptical and would voluntarily select primary care physicians in greater numbers if they had been invited to participate from the beginning.

Medicaid recipients have a number of specific concerns, and they intend to sue the state if appropriate action is not taken to meet them. Initially the inability to express dissatisfaction with a physician by switching to another provider disturbs many clients. This issue has been resolved, as noted above. Recipients are also fearful that the primary care physicians participating in the program cannot take appropriate care of some specialized or chronic problems, such as cystic fibrosis, but will not refer the patients because the physicians would lose money by doing so. Some recipients complain, too, that they must travel too far to their assigned primary care physician.

Consumer groups' foremost concern is one expressed as well by many physicians, other providers, and state officials. The Citicare feature of sharing financial risk with the physicians, which is designed to minimize overutilization, could also lead to underutilization. Recipients worry that they might be barred from receiving appropriate care.

To ensure that funds are not saved at the expense of appropriate care for its beneficiaries, the Jefferson County Medical Society established a quality-of-care committee in cooperation with Citicare. The idea was that the committee would monitor the quality of care delivered under the program, as well as inappropriate, insufficient, or excessive use of services. The committee has been slow in developing its approach to quality assessment, and details of how the monitoring system will function were still not apparent after the first twelve months of Citicare's operation.

Implications for Cost Containment

A university consortium, consisting of faculty members from both the University of Kentucky and the University of Louisville, is studying the effect of Citicare on utilization, costs, patient satisfaction, and quality of care. The study group has already collected base-line data through a consumer survey for the period before implementation in July 1983. It will conduct the survey again after the first year. The ongoing evaluation should help Citicare, Inc., to make any changes in program design that may become necessary. Although data from the consortium will not be available for some time, the following sections discuss the possible implications of Citicare for emergency room use, "abusive" physicians, and hospital use and present the first crude estimates of its utilization effects.

Emergency Room Use. Because many Medicaid recipients have no personal physician, they often use emergency rooms even when their problems do not require such a high level of medical sophistication. Overuse of costly emergency rooms has long been a major problem in Medicaid programs across the country.

Citicare links recipients directly with primary care providers, improving access to medical care and potentially reducing unnecessary visits to emergency rooms, as well as greatly decreasing "doctor shopping" (visits to multiple providers for the same problem) by recipients. Preliminary data from the first six months of Citicare's operation indicate that emergency room use has declined 53 percent from previous levels.

Under Citicare, the primary care providers must authorize all visits to emergency rooms unless the situation is life threatening. Participating physicians have a financial incentive in playing the gatekeeper role because payment for the professional portion of the emergency room visits comes directly from the physician's allocation for referral services fund. If the use of emergency rooms is too high, physicians will not be paid the remainder of their full capitation at the end of the year.

The financial incentive for minimizing emergency room use, however, must be balanced with the convenience of having patients seen and evaluated during the night and other off hours when the primary care physician is not in his office. Citicare doctors may not want to change their habits for possible extra profits some time in the future.

Another problem might come from emergency room physicians who fear liability charges if they withhold services from patients. Even if such hospital-based physicians understand Citicare policies, they may choose to treat the Medicaid recipients and shift costs to other payers rather than to turn patients away.

"Abusive" Physicians. Physicians who see many patients quickly and then refer them to specialists for care or prescribe more than the

49

average number of tests are regarded by the Medicaid program as "abusive." Some of these physicians in effect operate "Medicaid mills" and obtain their revenues by ordering multiple follow-up office visits as well as excessive tests and procedures.

The Citicare program limits the number of Medicaid recipients who can enroll with an individual physician to 1,800. This number serves only as a guideline, however, and it is not legally binding. Kentucky did not want to risk a lawsuit similar to the one in Michigan, which charged that limitations on patient loads damaged physicians' ability to earn a living. Nevertheless, Kentucky was sued on these grounds by a small number of physicians who lost. In any case, a regulation on the maximum number of enrolled patients per provider is unlikely by itself to have much effect on abusive physicians. Such a rule does not affect the basic practice patterns of physicians for whatever number of patients they actually treat.

Under Citicare the prepaid capitation that each primary care physician receives is the incentive for giving appropriate levels of care. If the physician orders numerous follow-up visits, he receives no additional income; all primary care is included in the established capitation rate. If the primary care provider refers patients too often to specialists, his allocation for the referral services fund will be more quickly depleted. If a physician renders too few services, patients may become sicker at a later date. When the referral services fund is exhausted, additional expenditures come from the hospital withholding fund, and the depletion of these funds eventually results in fewer dollars for the primary care physician.

Abusive physicians, therefore, simply lose money under the risk-sharing mechanisms of Citicare. The decrease in emergency room use indicates that physicians have changed their practice patterns in the expected direction. Physician visits increased approximately 16 percent in the first six months of Citicare in comparison with the same six months the year before. A majority of the physicians regarded as abusive derive most of their income from their Medicaid patients, and they are unlikely to jeopardize their livelihoods by continuing poor practice patterns.

Although the primary care physicians are not at risk for overuse of laboratory tests under Citicare, they cannot gain financially by such ordering patterns either. Citicare contracts for laboratory tests on a negotiated price and volume basis. The volume of laboratory tests may not decline under the program, but the bulk-ordering system should result in substantial savings on prices.

The necessity of approving or disapproving retroactive payment claims from specialists may be a continuing problem for Citicare. Patients who are not well informed about the system may continue to refer themselves to specialists. Moreover, all Louisville physicians have not been educated about the program. The general dissatisfaction in the medical community with the concept of prepayment and lack of direct access to specialists may make it difficult from a public relations standpoint for participating physicians to disapprove specialists' retroactive claims.

Hospital Use. Physicians have an incentive to hold down hospital costs because any institutional expenses that cannot be covered through the hospital management reserve come from the physicians' hospital withhold fund. Moreover, under the prepayment system, the physician receives the same compensation for his professional services regardless of whether he sees a patient a few times in his office or many times during a lengthy hospital stay. It is therefore in the financial interest of the physicians participating in Citicare to decrease admissions and to shorten lengths of stay in hospitals.

The AFDC beneficiaries in the program are generally healthy women and children. The problems that lead to hospitalization usually relate to pregnancy and childbearing for the women and respiratory and digestive ailments for the children. To reduce hospital use, Citicare physicians could try to avoid hospitalization whenever possible and treat conditions on an outpatient basis. Some procedures, such as circumcision, could quite easily be moved to an outpatient setting like an ambulatory surgery clinic. The university pediatricians, who are establishing two clinics, point out that with their new twenty-four-hour coverage, intravenous feedings can be given outside the hospital to dehydrated children with diarrhea. And even for deliveries, an outpatient alternative now exists. Several of the community health centers participating in Citicare have indicated interest in contracting for normal deliveries with birthing centers, although the centers are having difficulties identifying an obstetrician willing to participate. For many of the AFDC mothers, however, admissions cannot be avoided because these women are often at high risk for complications at delivery. Physicians are exploring the feasibility of one-day stays in conjunction with the home assistance program.

Increased emphasis on preventive care and health education also helps keep beneficiaries out of hospitals. Citicare has budgeted for these purposes. Hypertension, for example, a particular problem in the black community, can be controlled with drugs. Patient compliance with the drug therapy, which has been poor in low-income groups, can be improved through appropriate education. Citicare is setting aside funds for a variety of health education programs.

Participating physician groups could also seek to control inpatient expenditures by negotiating with hospitals for special rates for their patients. In the past such special rates were not permitted because the contracts that hospitals held with Blue Cross prohibited the hospitals from offering lower rates to any other group. That contractual restriction is no longer in effect, but hospital administrators still may not be anxious to increase their Medicaid population because Medicaid already reimburses at lower levels than other payers. Some hospital administrators may actively discourage their medical staff from admitting Citicare patients.

The physicians who practice at the University Hospital and who make up the majority of participating physicians in Citicare are in a delicate situation. They are not as free as other physicians to exert leverage on the University Hospital administrators by moving their Citicare patients to another institution because they rely on the university for their teaching programs and part of their incomes. The teaching hospital, however, is the most expensive inpatient facility in the community. Nevertheless, since the inception of Citicare, the university pediatricians have begun to send simple cases to community hospitals in Louisville. Although their extensive university involvement makes it more difficult to reduce hospital costs under the Citicare program, some intermediate options, such as negotiating lower prices on a restricted number of beds in the teaching hospital, may be feasible in the long run for the university physicians.

The early indications are that Citicare has been successful in realizing its goal of lower hospital use. Citicare has compared its hospital use rates to those in the Medicaid management information system. Inpatient hospital days per thousand have decreased from 750 to 402, and average length of stay has declined from 7.9 to 3.9 days.

Lessons Learned

That Citicare has at least partially realized its goal of decreasing hospital and emergency room use suggests that it has been successful. Several lessons can be distilled from its experience for others pursuing similar goals.

Like the Michigan PPSP, Citicare began during a statewide fiscal crisis and the threat of bankruptcy at the University Hospital. These circumstances provided the necessary impetus to plan the program. A task force with members representing the community, the city and county boards of health, the private sector, and the state coalesced around the notion of a primary care network. There was strong support from the secretary of the Cabinet of Human Resources for a change; he hired staff experienced in alternative delivery systems from outside Kentucky and found them necessary budgetary support. Despite dire financial problems, planning was not brushed aside by the urgency for implementation. In fact, to the dismay of many, enrollment was delayed several times because the system had not yet been fully specified to the satisfaction of the planners.

Despite its complexity, Citicare experienced few insurmountable problems when it went into operation. The problems concerning data, auto assignment, and grievances that were encountered lasted a shorter time than in other programs. The staff of Citicare gave a great deal of attention to the technical details of the program. While this effort lessened operational problems substantially, it came, to some extent, at the expense of fully informing and cultivating some consumers (who later sued) and legislators who might later have become a constituency for the long-term survival of the program.

Epilogue

In June 1984 the secretary of the Cabinet of Human Resources announced that Kentucky would not renew Citicare's contract for a second year. Thus Citicare closed its doors on June 30, 1984. The official government reasons for the demise of Citicare are as follows:

· Statewideness: The state wishes to have a statewide Medicaid cost containment program. It believes that a prepaid primary care network, such as Citicare, can be implemented only in densely populated urban areas, not statewide. The state prefers to implement a statewide fee-for-service case management system.

· Cost savings: The state did not believe Citicare saved money and thought the administrative costs too high. It also believed that other cost containment measures implemented since Citicare would have more effect.

· Utilization: The state was concerned about complaints from patients and physicians that necessary specialty care was not being provided and was inaccessible.

To understand the decision to close Citicare, it is important to put these decisions in the proper perspective and to evaluate the stated reasons against Citicare's experience.

Citicare, a major initiative of the John Y. Brown administration, was implemented during his last six months as governor. The current governor, Martha Layne Collins, then lieutenant governor, ran in the Democratic primary against Grady Stumbo, secretary of the Cabinet of Human Resources and one of the original backers of the Citicare concept. Because Stumbo and Mayor Harvey Sloane of Louisville (the only other Democratic candidate for governor) were both physicians, health became a major issue in the primary. During this period newspapers widely reported Governor Collins's promise to close Citicare if elected. This news from the front-runner made implementation of Citicare controversial, and put it in the public eye. Although Citicare was implemented only as a demonstration, the Brown administration thought of it as a first step toward stimulating competition across the state.

Statewideness. While it is true that programs using capitation are easier to implement when the potential enrollment is large so that the financial risk can be spread across many providers, implementation of a statewide prepaid primary care network is by no means impossible. Such a system has actually been implemented in other states with large rural populations. Examples are Patient's Choice and the Arizona Physicians' Individual Practice Association, which function as part of the Arizona Health Care Cost Containment System (AHCCCS). In these models, risks are pooled for physicians across the state. Contracts for laboratory, pharmacy, and other services can often be negotiated at better rates than for programs limited to smaller areas because of the greater volume of patients.

Cost Savings. Although Citicare was limited to Jefferson County and was one of the first Medicaid prepayment demonstrations to go into operation, it achieved notable results. Statistics presented previously indicated large declines in emergency room use, hospital length of stay, and hospital days per thousand population and a modest increase in out-of-hospital visits to physicians. These data reflected experience during the first six months of Citicare in comparison with the same six months the year before under Medicaid. Data obtained from Medicaid management information systems on utilization before Citicare are subject to error, but these findings are of the magnitude reported by Luft and others for prepaid plans in the private sector. While there is no guarantee that the figures are precise or would be exactly maintained over time, it is very unlikely they are illusory and do not translate into some cost savings.

Since Citicare is reimbursed at 95 percent of the projected fee-for-service Medicaid cost, the state automatically saves 5 percent. Both the state and Citicare require preadmission certification for hospitalization, although Citicare implemented this provision first. The Citicare version is more stringent in that patients are followed each day in the hospital—a capacity the state does not have. The state contends that the effectiveness of its preadmission certification program implies that Citicare was overpaid and that Citicare's savings are overstated. While this could be true, theory suggests that the stricter the preadmission program, the greater the savings.

The contract between Citicare, Inc., and Health America stipulated that 7.8 percent of revenue be paid to Health America for administration of the program. Out of these funds Health America was to cover all administrative expenses, including salaries, rent, supplies, and data processing. Whether the cost was higher than the state would have incurred had it administered the program itself is unknown, since there are no comparative data available.

Comparable situations may help put these administrative costs in perspective. The Santa Barbara Health Initiative, a nonprofit entity, receives about 1.2 percent from the state of California to administer its primary care network. The Health Authority claims, however, that 1.2 percent is much too low and that its costs, as well as those of the state under Medi-Cal, are on the order of 5–6 percent. The contract between Citicare and Health America does not require Health America to provide financial statements (income, profit and loss). Therefore, whether Health America was earning profits or sustaining losses for administration of the program cannot be determined.

Citicare also shows a $3.5 million surplus in the hospital management reserve. The formula stipulated in the contract between Citicare and the state allocates this surplus one-third to the state, one-third to Citicare, and one-third to Health America—more than $1 million to each. The state's share alone constitutes an additional saving of almost 5 percent of the $22 million Citicare budget. Since Citicare has not been renewed, its portion of the savings will also revert to the state. Whether funds remaining in the hospital management reserve suggest overpayment to Citicare is arguable. To cut back on funding would have lessened the financial incentive for physicians to bring down hospital use and might have substantially reduced cost savings on hospitalization. While the relationship between the strength of the financial incentive and the amount of cost savings is not clear, it is clear that substantial incentives must exist for all parties to be motivated to make the program work.

Underutilization and Lack of Referrals. The state expressed concern over complaints from providers and consumers that referrals were often difficult to obtain. Such complaints are common in prepaid programs. The problem of monitoring underutilization is difficult because there is no agreement on how to measure it. Even though the Jefferson County Medical Society was not successful in implementing a quality assurance program, Citicare did implement utilization review and quality assurance programs of its own. One aspect of the quality assurance program was a formal grievance procedure. Since such procedures were not available under traditional Medicaid, it is impossible to compare the rate of grievances before and during Citicare. Theory would suggest, however, that more grievances will occur where a formal procedure exists.

The grievances filed by patients under Citicare were primarily of two types: complaints that physicians would not refer the patients to specialists and complaints that physicians were not treating patients courteously. Complaints were treated case by case by the medical director of Citicare. There were few grievances, and it became apparent that *only a few* physicians were the offenders. Citicare was in the midst of deciding what action to take on these physicians when the program was terminated.

5
The Santa Barbara
Health Initiative

California has long experimented with developing alternative health care delivery systems. As early as 1978, the state legislature passed a bill that provided seed money of $50,000 for counties and other agencies of government to develop experimental delivery systems that tackled the escalating costs of Medi-Cal, California's Medicaid program. Santa Barbara County was one of the first funded under this program in early 1980.

Development of the Health Initiative

County officials located the program, the Santa Barbara Health Initiative, in the county's Department of Health Care Services and convened a series of meetings with the local medical society to decide what kind of delivery system should be developed. They agreed that the initiative should be controlled at the local level rather than at the state level and that an organization independent of the county government should administer the program. With medical society endorsement and seed money from the state, additional funding was obtained from The John A. Hartford Foundation, and professional staff was hired to begin planning in late 1981.

Planning became mired in a struggle between Santa Barbara County and the state government over federal waivers. The state, which had received the waivers from the Health Care Financing Administration (HCFA) in the U.S. Department of Health and Human Services, refused to pass them on to Santa Barbara County. The state was concerned about the plan to guarantee eligibility for six months to patients enrolling in the new program and about Santa Barbara County's desire to use its own fiscal agent rather than the state's.

In March 1982, the state legislature resolved the problem by passing Assembly Bill 1223, which authorized the establishment of the Santa Barbara Special Health Care Authority (health authority), an independent public agency separate from county government. The independent agency was necessary since without it the county could not serve as a broker with itself (a major provider of services) or other providers without a conflict of interest. The legislation called for the health authority to operate an alternative delivery system providing all benefits under the Medi-Cal program for 95 percent of the costs that would have been incurred in the county under the fee-for-service system. During the same legislative session, another bill was passed exempting the health authority from regulation as a health maintenance organization (HMO) under the state's Knox-Keene Act, thus permitting the Health Initiative to operate without the reserves required of HMOs.

The Santa Barbara Special Health Care Authority has established a primary care network incorporating case management and capitation payments to providers. Its board, which was constituted according to its enabling legislation, includes physicians, consumers, hospital administrators, and local government officers appointed by the county board of supervisors. The Health Initiative began operations on September 1, 1983, and now covers 24,000 Medi-Cal beneficiaries in Santa Barbara County. All eligibility categories in the Medi-Cal program are covered by the Health Initiative, with the exception of 2000 medically indigent adults, the responsibility for whom was recently returned by the state to the county.

Operation of the Health Initiative

Physician Participation. The Santa Barbara Special Health Care Authority contracts for medical care and case management services with individual primary care physicians and the county's medical services. While the county department delivers a full spectrum of services to beneficiaries, financial risk is placed on the department only for primary care and specialty services. Social services and nutrition services, for example, have traditionally been considered county services, but they are not specifically covered under the capitation plan. Some health care providers within the department fear that the county will be unable to continue to provide some of these extra services without sufficient reimbursement to cover costs.

The county employs salaried physicians to provide primary care services at several sites. Specialty care is provided by the largest hospital in the city of Santa Barbara under contract to the county. No specialty services are available to enrollees in the county system in the rural or northern sections of the county. The county provides bus service twice weekly, but enrollees living in the northern part of the county must spend an entire day traveling in order to obtain services. The county maintains that it would be too expensive to provide specialty services in additional locations, but the single-site situation has created access problems for a number of beneficiaries using the county services.

A multispecialty group practice with considerable prestige, the Santa Barbara Medical Foundation Clinic, expressed early interest in serving as case manager. Late in the development of the initiative, however, the clinic decided not to participate. Its physicians feared that the sickest patients would be attracted to the clinic and the capitation payments would not cover such adverse selection since rates include no adjustment for health status. Like other specialists, the clinic has contracted with the health authority to provide specialty services on a fee-for-service basis only.

Currently about 350 of the 600 physicians in Santa Barbara County have individually contracted with the health authority to provide primary care and case management services to Medi-Cal beneficiaries. Many of these physicians signed with the health authority just when the program was beginning in September 1983 (rather than before), and beneficiaries were unable to select them when they enrolled during the previous July and August.

Initially the Health Initiative had poor participation by physicians during the enrollment period for several reasons. Originally each primary care physician had to be willing to accept an enrollment of at least 125 beneficiaries as a condition of participation. The health authority required the minimum enrollment so that an individual physician's financial risk would be minimized and capitation payments could be actuarially determined in a fair way. Many physicians did not fully understand the reasons for this provision, and they believed that accepting so many Medi-Cal patients would cause too much paper work and lower their overall incomes. In Santa Barbara County, no physician has an overwhelmingly large number of Medi-Cal patients. Most physicians see some beneficiaries, and they have continued to treat these patients under the new initiative.

To increase the participation of primary care physicians, the health authority changed the rule concerning minimum enrollment about a month before the initiative became operational. Physicians were still encouraged, but not required, to enroll a minimum of 125 Medi-Cal patients. To preserve the appropriate financial incentives and risk structure, primary care physicians who sponsor fewer than 125 patients must agree to share their risk with other physicians who similarly enroll fewer than 125 beneficiaries.

Because of a misunderstanding about the hold-harmless provision that they are required to sign with the health authority, many physicians believed that the authority's liability would be shifted to the physicians. The intent of the provision, however, was to have the state "held harmless" in the event that the authority becomes insolvent. The California Medical Association had previously counseled physicians not to sign contracts with hold-harmless clauses. As a result, at first several groups of specialists, particularly urologists, ophthalmologists, orthopedists, and neurosurgeons, refused to join the Health Initiative; when the program started in September 1983, no physicians from these specialties were under contract to the health authority. The confusion surrounding this provision was finally dispelled.

The position of the county medical society also contributed to the initial poor participation by physicians. During the planning stages it had endorsed the Health Initiative, but before the operational phase it withdrew its support. There were several reasons for the medical society's switch. Most important were reimbursement changes by the Medi-Cal program that were unrelated to the Health Initiative. In 1982 the state sharply reduced fees for physicians under Medi-Cal. Physicians in the community had been hesitant to take Medi-Cal patients before the fee cuts, and the additional reductions fueled fears that even more cuts would be made in the future under the health authority. The physicians were reluctant to endorse a plan that they believed eroded both their earning capacity and their ability to conduct their practices freely.

Moreover, there was a misunderstanding about the medical society's role in the Health Initiative. The health authority first presented the initiative to the medical society as a plan that would increase the timeliness of payments to physicians, reduce paper work, promote cost-effective medicine, and be locally administered. Based on this presentation, the board of directors of the county medical society formed a study group to help design the plan. Although the structure and organization of the program had not been defined, most community physicians thought it would take the form of an IPA, similar to the Redwood Foundation for Medical Care, under which the functions of the fiscal intermediary and utilization review were assumed by the medical society. Thus the medical society believed it would have direct responsibility for operating the plan. When the Health Initiative took the different direction of a primary care network, the physicians felt deceived.

It is difficult to assess how important the lack of endorsement by the medical society was in determining physicians' participation in the Health Initiative. It is true that many physicians who later signed with the health authority were not under contract when beneficiaries chose or were assigned primary care physicians. Some younger physicians, seeking to build their practices, profited by the nonparticipation of established providers. Because few doctors were available during the enrollment period, these young physicians who had contracted with the health authority were assigned to or were chosen by as many as 100–300 new patients. The capitation amounts that they collected from the health authority were far greater than the fees they had previously been receiving under the Medi-Cal program. Cognizant of these problems, the health authority has since allowed beneficiaries to change primary care physicians during the first two months of the program so that they may sign with the physician of their choice.

Incentives for Cost Containment. The state pays the health authority 95 percent of the projected fee for service cost for each eligible recipient. The specific capitation amount is adjusted by aid category but not by health status, age, or sex. The state's payment is called the full capitation. The health authority creates an account for each primary care physician. Each month the health care authority credits the primary care physician or some contracting entity account with a percentage of the full capitation amount paid by the state for each enrolled recipient by aid category. The full capitation is then divided into several trust accounts (risk pools) for primary care services, specialty care, hospital services, ancillary services (X-ray and laboratory), pharmacy, and durable medical equipment.

Both primary care physicians who contract directly with the health authority and the county accept risk by receiving only a portion of the full monthly capitation to compensate them for all care delivered to Medi-Cal beneficiaries. But the amount of this capitation is slightly different for these two categories of providers. The health authority pays 80 percent of the monthly primary care capitation directly to the primary care physician in advance and withholds the remaining 20 percent as a risk pool. Out of these funds, the physicians are required to provide all necessary primary care. Regardless of the number of primary care services provided, the primary care physician is guaranteed the full 80 percent.

By way of contrast, the county is at somewhat greater risk than the independent primary care physicians because it must provide or pay for all covered outpatient services, not only primary care, out of its capitation payments. No portion of the capitation is withheld to create an additional risk pool, and, of course, the county is at risk for outpatient and specialty services as well as for primary care services. If expenses exceed payments, the health authority provides no further funds. If the county has a surplus at the end of the year, however, it shares that surplus 50/50 with the health authority.

All specialists are paid at prevailing reimbursement rates established by the Medi-Cal program. They are reimbursed only if a participating primary care physician authorizes their services. Under the terms of the program, specialists are also expected to sign the hold-harmless provision that the health authority requires. All authorized specialty care is debited against the specialty care risk pool, money for which is set aside out of the full capitation at the beginning of each month. In addition, terms of the program permit primary care physicians to provide specialty services, which are also reimbursed on a fee-for-service basis out of the specialty risk pool. Specific California relative value study codes define the specialty and primary care services covered under the 80 percent of the primary care capitation paid to primary care physicians. Early indications are that primary care physicians do provide many specialty services and that they believe that this is a way to guarantee themselves income. Some are skeptical that the 20 percent withheld will ever be returned to them.

The primary care physicians must approve all pharmacy, laboratory, and durable equipment purchases which are reimbursed at prevailing Medi-Cal fee-for-service rates. All payments are debited to the appropriate trust accounts.

The health authority pays hospitals an all-inclusive per diem rate. Negotiated with the hospitals in the community, the rate must be less than the rate the Medi-Cal program would have paid. The per diem rate includes all routine and ancillary costs of the hospital. (In 1982 the state started a program to contract selectively with hospitals under Medi-Cal. The state has empowered a Medi-Cal "czar" to negotiate favorable per diem rates with providers. The czar was replaced by a commission in 1984.) Technically the initiative is exempt, but the all-inclusive rate negotiated by the health authority cannot exceed what would have been negotiated by the czar.

Because a general goal of the health authority is to increase the speed of payments to providers, the hospitals are to receive 50 percent of their anticipated reimbursement in advance and the rest monthly. The health authority recalculates the payments each month on the basis of the previous month's utilization experience. Payments and charges are reconciled at the end of the year.

The legislation, which established the health authority, mandated that the health authority offer a contract to each of the eight hospitals in Santa Barbara County, but there were no stipulations that the contracts be signed. Problems have arisen with the way that the rates are calculated, and some hospitals are dissatisfied with the method of payment.

The all-inclusive per diem rate is based on the previous cost and utilization experience of each hospital. During the development of the Health Initiative, the health authority hired an actuary to analyze data from the hospitals, the California Health Facilities Commission, and the CSC Corporation, the Medi-Cal fiscal agent. There was significant disagreement among the data sources on per unit cost. The hospitals, for example, apparently systematically overestimated days of care.

Concerned over rates, the hospitals requested representation on the health authority's board. Two hospital administrators were appointed who negotiated general provisions and principles for the hospital contracts. The health authority refined the actuary's initial estimates to reflect new assumptions that the hospitals had introduced.

Each hospital was supposed to negotiate its own contract with the health authority. In fact, the authority offered each hospital a per diem rate that the authority itself calculated. Six of the eight community hospitals reluctantly accepted the rate offered by the health authority because it was made clear that no additional funds would be available. The other two hospitals succeeded in getting their rates adjusted slightly upward. Had both hospitals not signed, significant access problems for patients in the north county would have resulted.

The hospitals believe that the state's budgetary constraints on the health authority have unfairly penalized them. Not only were they forced to accept rates lower than those initially promised, but also it took forty-five days to make the first payments to the hospitals at the beginning of the Health Initiative. Hence hospitals believe they have lost a substantial amount of money promised them.

At the end of the year, the authority settles all trust accounts and presents an accounting showing debits and credits. First, each trust fund is reconciled. For all *except* the primary care trust fund, trust fund savings are split equally between the primary care physician and the health authority. If there are losses in these other trust accounts because debits exceed credits, losses are paid first out of the 20 percent withheld for primary care services. In this way primary care physicians are at risk for services they authorize but do not deliver out of their capitation. If the independent primary care physicians' 20 percent withholding account is depleted, the health authority pays any remainder out of its required reserves. The State Division of Health Services requires that the health authority keep one month's capitation in reserve. In the event that any of the 20 percent withhold remains at the end of the year, it is returned to the primary care physician. Physicians who have surpluses (or losses) in their 20 percent withhold account will have less (or more) money withheld from their primary care capitation in succeeding years.

Other providers of limited services, such as psychologists, optometrists, podiatrists, chiropractors, acupuncturists, and faith healers, are paid under the usual methods of the Medi-Cal program. Their services do not have to be authorized by the primary care physicians; but, under the regulations of the Medi-Cal program, payment for their services is subject to limitations. Pharmacists are also paid in the usual way under the Medi-Cal program, but the participating physicians must write or authorize prescriptions for recipients enrolled in the Health Initiative.

Administration. The Santa Barbara Special Health Care Authority receives its funds from the state Medi-Cal program, and, in turn, pays providers. The state's per capita costs are calculated by aid category, and adjusted downward 5 percent. Thus the state pays the health authority only 95 percent of what the state's expenses would have been under the fee-for-service system for the enrolled Medi-Cal beneficiaries.

The health authority allocates the funds to specific accounts for primary care physicians, the county, hospitals, specialist services, laboratories, and so forth. Each account is its own risk pool. The health authority also maintains a risk reserve account to protect against unanticipated losses. The risk reserve covers the health authority's expenses for individual catastrophic illnesses (all expenses between the primary care physician's capitation and the state's coverage of expenses over $15,000).

The full capitation consists of all the capitation payments to physicians, the partial capitation to counties, and payments for inpatient and outpatient hospital services, specialists' services, and ancillary services. In addition, there are required reserves for limited services (for example, psychology, optometry, and chiropody) and institutional population medical services for long-term care. The grand total cannot exceed the aggregate capitation amount that the health authority receives from the state.

The health authority also receives additional funds from the state to cover the expenses of certain categories of Medi-Cal beneficiaries whose care is reimbursed on a fee-for-service basis (class two beneficiaries). Any provider who has a contract with the health authority can give care to these beneficiaries after receiving authorization from the medical director of the authority. Reimbursement is at the prevailing fee-for-service rates used by the Medi-Cal program. These fee-for-service rates for the disabled and institutionalized populations are separate from capitation for class one beneficiaries (defined below), and therefore insulate primary care physicians from substantial financial risk.

This combination of both capitation and fee-for-service reimbursement requires continual data collection and manipulation for program management. Because the Santa Barbara Special Health Care Authority did not have sufficient capabilities or resources within its own staff, it awarded a fixed-price contract to Jurgovan and Blair, Inc. (JBI), to serve as a fiscal agent. Thus JBI, which was selected competitively, also shares with the health authority the risk of cost overruns. The fiscal agent is responsible for processing enrollment and disenrollment forms and for designing the random assignment procedures used during the initial enrollment process. It pays the providers, including physicians and hospitals, and reconciles all accounts. JBI also produces a variety of management reports based on the data collected.

To hire a contractor to administer a large project of this kind is unusual. The health authority wanted the expertise of the fiscal agent, particularly the ability to design computer software for the program. In addition, the outside agent had to have sufficient capital, which the health authority seemed to lack, to purchase necessary computer hardware.

Because many aspects of the program were not finalized until the initiative became operational, JBI was delayed in developing software and installing hardware. One problem concerned the format and content of the patient-encounter form, the mechanism for tracking physician visits and other health care events. The health authority wanted the form to facilitate program monitoring and, at the same time, to be easy for physicians to complete. Eventually the health authority decided to develop a new encounter form but to continue using the CSC form supplied by the Medi-Cal program for billing purposes. JBI's location in Santa Rosa, California, made initial communications difficult, but JBI opened an office in Santa Barbara shortly after the Health Initiative began operations.

In addition to the fiscal agent, the health authority has hired a medical director. The medical director serves as the case manager for all those beneficiaries whose care is reimbursed on a fee-for-service basis. The director is also in charge of the quality-assurance program and must approve all hospitalizations that the physicians participating in the program authorize. Basically the prior authorization procedures used in the Medi-Cal program for hospitalizations and elective surgeries are used in the Health Initiative as well. Any elective procedure that Medi-Cal does not cover the Health Initiative does not permit either. Many physicians had hoped that utilization review would become the purview of the medical society under the Health Initiative. Budget constraints and other factors led, however, to retention of the Medi-Cal program's procedures and restrictions.

The health authority receives 1.2 percent of health expenditures as reimbursement for administrative costs from the state. Originally the health authority believed it would receive 6 to 7 percent, the equivalent of what it costs the state for administration of Medi-Cal. The state did not wish to pay more since it believed it would still have substantial fixed costs. JBI is paid out of these funds. Neither party believes the dispute was adequately settled.

Beneficiary Enrollment. Enrollment in the Santa Barbara Health Initiative is mandatory for all beneficiaries in the county (in all aid categories) who are eligible for Medi-Cal. Class one patients include AFDC recipients and account for about 85 percent of all Medi-Cal eligibles. All class one beneficiaries are required to select a primary care physician to serve as case manager. Class two patients, who make up the remaining 15 percent of Medi-Cal eligibles, include recipients who are in long-term care facilities, are disabled, are required to share in the costs of their own care, or are on renal dialysis. These patients often have complex health care problems, and a single primary care physician cannot appropriately function as their case manager. Class two patients are automatically assigned to the medical director of the Santa Barbara Special Health Care Authority who serves as their case manager.

Traditionally, the bulk of care for AFDC beneficiaries consists of prenatal care, deliveries, and well-child care. Hence, expenditures are predictable and are likely to be low in comparison with those for individuals in other aid categories whose medical needs are greater and more complex. On the margin, the most money can be saved through primary care case management for class two beneficiaries. The removal of these individuals from the capitated case management system shelters all primary care physicians from adverse risk selection. Although this measure may have been necessary to guarantee the participation of physicians in adequate numbers, substantial cost savings are likely to be forgone.

During the summer of 1983 the health authority sent a letter to all class one Medi-Cal recipients describing the Health Initiative. In this letter, beneficiaries were asked to choose a primary care physician from a list of those physicians participating in the program. If the recipient did not make a selection, the health authority sent a reminder. If there still was no response, a primary care physician was randomly assigned to each beneficiary. This procedure assigned patients to primary care physicians according to a formula that accounts for the age and zip code of the patient. An attempt was made to match patients to primary care physicians suitable for the patient's age group (for example, forty-five-year-old adults were not assigned to pediatricians) and located close to the patient's residence. Unfortunately, during the early stages of the program, there were many problems with the assignment formulas. In particular, specialties were misassigned. Men, for example, were assigned to gynecologists. The health authority resolved the problems with the assignment system.

Although responsibility for eligibility determination for AFDC beneficiaries rests with the county welfare department, JBI performs the enrollment and selection procedures. This division of responsibility between eligibility determination and enrollment has created substantial implementation problems. The major problem is obtaining accurate eligibility data for enrollment. Because eligibility status under Medi-Cal changes frequently for many recipients, it is important that enrollment be based on up-to-date data. Eligibility is not guaranteed for a given time under the Health Initiative, and data provided by the county welfare department have not been sufficiently timely.

The first enrollment mailing, which took place in August, was based on July eligibility data. As a result, recipients who had lost their eligibility by August were asked to select primary care physicians, and beneficiaries who were newly eligible for Medi-Cal in August were unable to participate in the program. Thus access to care was difficult for a few very sick patients.

Implications for Cost Containment

In the area of cost containment the goals of the Santa Barbara Health Initiative are to reduce admissions and lengths of stay in hospitals and to reduce unnecessary emergency room visits. The primary mechanisms to accomplish these goals are the case management system, under which the primary care physicians serve as gatekeepers to specialty care and hospitalization, and the inclusive per diem rates that are negotiated with the hospitals.

It is not clear what effect the case management system will have on hospital admissions. The physicians participating in the Health Initiative receive capitation payments for primary care services, but they are not directly at financial risk for hospital services. They are only indirectly at risk in that their withhold subsidizes the hospital risk pool if it is depleted. Thus, although they have accepted the responsibility of managing all their patients' medical care, they may not benefit or lose financially from their actions except as these actions affect the care that they render themselves. Under the Health Initiative, prior authorization by the medical director of the Santa Barbara Special Health Care Authority is also required for any hospitalization. This procedure, rather than the incentive structure, will probably control hospital admissions. Similarly, negotiated hospital rates rather than incentives will probably curb hospital expenditures.

The hospitals are paid an all-inclusive per diem rate for patients enrolled in the Health Initiative. Because the rate is lower than the hospitals might receive from charge-paying patients, there may be some incentive to avoid admitting Medi-Cal patients. Once the beneficiaries are hospitalized, however, the incentive is to lengthen their stay, since the hospital is reimbursed the same amount for each day of hospitalization regardless of the resources the patients consume.

Only primary care physicians are supposed to authorize emergency room care if the need for medical care is not life threatening. Some of the participating physicians have indicated that gradual education will be necessary for patients who frequently turn first to the emergency rooms for care. These providers anticipate authorizing the emergency room care the first few times their patients go, but they plan to contact the patients immediately and set up office appointments so that the behavior does not continue.

The staff of the emergency rooms may also present a problem. Emergency room physicians may be reluctant to turn patients away, particularly since differentiating true emergencies from non-life-threatening cases is often difficult. No specific education about the Health Initiative is now provided for emergency room personnel. The case management system will likely have an effect on emergency room use, but the decrease in use probably will be gradual.

Participating primary care physicians must authorize all specialty care, though they are not at direct financial risk for their referrals (for example, they do not have to pay for specialty services directly). When a patient needs to be seen by a specialist, the primary care provider completes a referral form and sends it to the health authority and the specialist. A copy is also given to the patient. The form allows referrals to be made for any length of time or for any number of episodes. Such blanket referrals are generally considered to be cost raising rather than cost saving. There are now no plans to penalize the primary care physicians who make more referrals than their peers.

Several other issues concerning the organization of the health authority could affect its success or failure in dealing with health care costs. Originally, when the federal Health Care Financing Administration granted waivers to the state, the federal government and the state understood that Santa Barbara County would be responsible for operating the program and receiving the Medi-Cal funds from the state. Instead the legislature established the Santa Barbara Special Health Care Authority, which is separate from the county government but is the legal broker for contracting with providers and beneficiaries.

The quandary arises that if the state's Medi-Cal payments are insufficient to cover all the health authority's expenses, what entity is at risk? In theory, the health authority assumed the county's obligations when it was established, and it would be at risk for any shortfalls between the capitations it pays out and the reinsurance that the state pays for losses over $15,000 per enrollee. Although not yet tested, the health authority may not be legally responsible because it has no assets. If this proves to be the case, physicians and other providers would be unable to sue the health authority. Practically, this issue could become a problem if it decreases providers' confidence in the Health Initiative.

Another potential problem concerns the state's funding of the health authority. Currently the state pays $25 million to cover the 24,000 eligible Medi-Cal beneficiaries in Santa Barbara County. The health authority budgets only 3 percent to 4 percent of these funds for administration of the program. Most similar programs have allowed 8 percent or 9 percent of total revenues for administration. This perceived under-funding has made some members of the board of directors skeptical about the health authority's ability to deliver services to its Medi-Cal beneficiaries within the budgetary constraints imposed by the state.

Lessons Learned

Unlike the three other programs discussed in this book, the Santa Barbara Health Initiative was planned and implemented by a local group without significant resources (human or monetary) from the state. In retrospect, the decision to develop the program as a local effort had several advantages and disadvantages for implementation.

It meant early support from the medical society and ample participation by primary care physicians. Consumers became actively involved in planning and implementation through their representation on an elected board; so did hospitals, which negotiated with the authority collectively. But the local influence was still not enough to counteract the hesitation of certain subspecialists to join or to persuade new leadership of the medical society not to withdraw its support. Although, as I have suggested elsewhere in the book, it is unlikely that any program can generate unanimous support, local administration can get all interest groups together easily and work toward resolution of existing problems.

As in Kentucky, the county health officer for Santa Barbara strongly supported the program and committed the necessary resources to hire an individual experienced with alternative delivery systems to head the planning effort. He was then able to secure outside funding to hire staff and ensure the soundness of the technical approach.

Many of the early implementation problems (all of which were eventually solved) stemmed from a lack of communication and understanding between the state and county. Among them were the hesitancy of the state to pass on waivers from HCFA because the state did not approve the protocol of the program, a lack of agreement regarding the appropriate reimbursement for administrative costs, and a lack of coordination between eligibility and enrollment functions. Intergovernmental relations are always difficult. But an integrated, planned effort involving all parties is critical if a complicated and innovative program such as the Santa Barbara Health Initiative is to be successful.

Other early problems resulted from inexperience with contracting for the services of a fiscal agent. In particular, the fiscal agent was given very little time to develop the software programs necessary to support the claims payment and routine reporting functions. It appears to be necessary for the fiscal agent to have experience in a prepaid environment and for the claims processing and quality assurance functions to be planned in advance. In these ways, smooth administration of the program is much more likely.

6
Summary: A Comparison of Program Characteristics

The case studies have demonstrated the variety of motives that lead states to institute more competitive delivery systems and to choose various program features. Yet for all the differences, there are similarities among programs as well. Table 2 presents a comparison of program characteristics, to highlight similarities and differences and help the interested administrator design a program most suited to local needs. The discussion of program characteristics has been divided into eight broad categories: (1) governance and organizational form; (2) plan administration; (3) physicians and health plans; (4) hospitals; (5) consumer involvement; (6) utilization review and quality assurance; (7) enrollment; and (8) marketing.

Governance and Organizational Form

In some instances, plans are governed by a steering committee or by a board of directors. In Michigan a steering committee includes some physicians and osteopaths who sponsor the program. In Santa Barbara a board of directors composed of elected representatives supervises and sets policy for the Santa Barbara Special Health Care Authority.

All of the programs are designed to use a primary care physician who acts as a gatekeeper to needed medical services, and are, therefore, described as primary care networks. These primary care networks frequently involve physicians in private solo practice and fee-for-service group practice, as well as physicians in independent practice associations (IPAs) and health maintenance organizations (HMOs). All physicians involved must agree to deliver care according to the concept of a primary care gatekeeper.

These programs have various sponsors, including governments at the state and local levels and medical societies. Although the Santa Barbara Health Initiative was conceived within the county government, the health authority that runs the program is an independent,

TABLE 2
Comparison of Four Health Programs

	Michigan: Primary Physician Sponsor Plan (Wayne County)	Utah Choice of Health Care Plan (Salt Lake, Weber Utah Counties)	Kentucky: Citicare Plan (Jefferson County)	California: Santa Barbara Health Initiative (Santa Barbara County)
Governance and organizational form				
Board of directors	Yes	No	No	Yes
Type	PCN	PCN	PCN	PCN
Sponsorship	Medical society	State	State	County
Projected number of enrollees	280,000	38,000	40,000	24,000
Eligibility categories covered	AFDC[a]	All	AFDC	All except medically indigent adults
Voluntary (V)/Mandatory (M)	M	V	M	M
Percentage enrolled if voluntary	NA	92	NA	NA
Plan administration				
Contract managed by fiscal agent	No	No	Yes	Yes
Fiscal agent at risk	NA	NA	Yes	Yes
Fiscal agent for-profit, nonprofit	NA	NA	For-profit	For-profit
State provides stop loss	NA	NA	No	Yes
Rates set by outside actuary	NA	NA	No	Yes
Physicians and health plans				
24-hour coverage required	Yes	Yes	Yes	Yes
Primary care physician payment mode	Fee-for-service	Fee-for-service	Capitation	Capitation

Primary care physician at risk	Yes	No	Yes	Yes
Extent of risk/loss of participation	Loss of participation	NA	Profits, losses	Profits
Specialist payment mode	Fee-for-service	Fee-for-service	Fee-for-service	Fee-for-service
Specialists at risk	No	No	No	No
Maximum number of patients per PCP	2,000	None	1,800	None
Minimum number of patients per PCP	None	None	300	125
Medical school participation	Yes	Yes	Yes	NA
Percentage of enrollees in HMOs	25	25	5	None
Number of HMOs	7	1	1	None
Referral form required for specialist payment	No	Yes	Yes	Yes
Primary care physician at risk for hospitalization	No	No	Yes	No
Hospitals				
Prior authorization required	Yes	Yes	Yes	Yes
Responsibility for prior authorization	Primary care physician	Primary care physician	Primary care physician	County
Payment mode	Standard Medicaid	Standard Medicaid	Standard Medicaid	All-inclusive rates
Hospital at risk	No	No	No	No
Consumer involvement				
Involved in plan design	Yes	Yes	No	Yes
Guaranteed eligibility	No	No	No	No
Welfare rights groups active	Yes	Yes	Yes	No
Impending law suits	Yes	No	Yes	No
Utilization review and quality assurance				
Responsibility for UR	State	State	Administrator	Administrator
Responsibility for QA	Medical society, state	State	Medical society	Administrator

(Table continues)

TABLE 2 (continued)

	Michigan: Primary Physician Sponsor Plan (Wayne County)	Utah: Choice of Health Care Plan (Salt Lake, Weber Utah Counties)	Kentucky: Citicare Plan (Jefferson County)	California: Santa Barbara Health Initiative (Santa Barbara County)
Enrollment				
Department responsible for enrollment	Social services	Health services	Social services	Administrator
Same department as responsible for eligibility	Yes	No	Yes	No
Phase-in period	2 months	1 year	2 months	2 months
Linked to recertification	No	Yes	No	No
Enrollment method	Telephone	Personal interview	Personal interview	Mailing
Type of personnel	Social worker	Health worker	Social worker	Social worker
Marketing				
Mailings	Yes	Yes	Yes	Yes
Community Meetings	Yes	Yes	Yes	Yes

NOTE: NA = not applicable; PCN = primary care network; AFDC = aid to families with dependent children; PCP = primary care physician.
a. The PPSP includes some disability insurance recipients; all other groups are excluded.
SOURCE: Author.

quasi-governmental agency.

An important factor in the success or failure of these programs is the number of beneficiaries that can be enrolled; all of the plans expect to enroll a large number of eligible individuals. The expected number of enrollees is largely a function of the number of eligibility categories covered and of whether the plan is mandatory or voluntary. In many instances the number of eligibility categories covered was of particular concern, affecting the viability of the plans and the amount of money that could be saved. Covering fewer patients in the earlier stages, for example, would allow for ease of implementation but would lessen the cost-saving potential.

For the foreseeable future, most states will concentrate on enrolling only mothers and children eligible for Aid to Families with Dependent Children (AFDC), although most states will later try to enroll other eligibility categories. The reasons for including only AFDC recipients are varied, but in most instances AFDC recipients were chosen because they constitute the largest group, their eligibility is fairly stable, and their health care expenses can be easily predicted so that it is easier to devise capitation rates for them.

Some states have decided to make their case management system for the primary care network mandatory for all eligible persons in a particular county. This decision is not easy to make, and it is generally made for political reasons. The most important factor in choosing a mandatory plan is the urgent need to save money. Two of the three states selecting mandatory enrollment (Michigan and Kentucky) were in a severe recession at the time the decision was made. Voluntary plans are generally implemented because physician backlash or citizen protest is great, but they also appear to be more easily implemented. One voluntary enrollment plan has, in fact, been marketed quite successfully in competition against the traditional Medicaid fee-for-service program and has enrolled 92 percent of the eligible population within a year of its initiation.

Plan Administration

The manner of implementation and the responsibility for daily operation often vary across plans. This section briefly describes different ways that plans are administered and provides some explanation of why states have chosen a particular method of administration.

The two sites, Kentucky and Santa Barbara County, California, that have chosen prepayment programs have also chosen to contract for administrative services. All responsibility for administering the Kentucky plan rests with an outside organization that was competitively selected. In Santa Barbara the role of the outside contractor, which was also competitively selected, is primarily limited to enrollment and to the traditional responsibilities of a fiscal agent, such as paying claims and collecting data. Contracts with physicians and negotiations with hospitals are carried out by the Santa Barbara health authority. The correlation between prepayment and the decision to have an outside contractor as fiscal agent is unclear, but states with prepayment plans have noted that an outside administrator has greater flexibility to hire staff and purchase equipment and provides expertise often not available within the state or county governments.

Both of the sites with an outside contractor have also chosen to put the contractor at some financial risk, although the way in which they structure the risk is different. In both cases the contractor was offered financial incentives to administer the plan within the budget. In Santa Barbara the outside contractor/fiscal agent was hired before plan operations began. Furthermore, the contractor was asked to risk start-up money for the development of computer and billing systems even before it was certain that the Santa Barbara Health Initiative would become operational.

Both outside contractors are for-profit organizations, but it is interesting to note their backgrounds and experience. Almost all of the contract bids were filed by firms that had had significant experience processing Medicaid claims. In fact, some of the firms were then serving as the Medicaid fiscal intermediary. The winning contractors in Kentucky and California, however, were firms with extensive prepayment experience rather than extensive experience in Medicaid claims payment. The program sponsors seemed to recognize the importance of providing the program with expertise in prepayment plans, particularly in prepayment plans with poorer populations.

Of considerable concern to any provider participating in a primary care network is the potential for one catastrophic event to erase whatever profits have been accumulated. The two programs that have chosen prepayment have tried to solve this problem differently. Santa Barbara has devised a stop-loss provision that limits an individual provider's risk to $15,000 per patient in expenditures; the state is responsible for any expenditures in excess of $15,000. In Kentucky the contracted administrator is asked to reinsure and provide stop-loss insurance for all physician expenditures over $5,000 per patient.

Determining a rate that will guarantee cost savings and at the same time be fair to participants is another difficult task, and states have approached this problem in different ways. Santa Barbara chose to contract with an outside actuary to calculate rates. In Kentucky individuals responsible for hospital and physician rate setting in the traditional Medicaid program set the program payment levels. It is too early to speculate on how accurate the rates are or whether accuracy has increased by using an outside actuary. It is certain, however, that the capitation rates depend substantially on the availability of adequate base-line data, on detailed information about how the plan will operate, and on assumptions about utilization. If plans cannot be described in detail at the time the actuary is brought in, utilization assumptions are often incorrect, and the rates are suspect.

Physicians and Health Plans

Within each plan, primary care physicians and specialists are reimbursed differently, and they have different financial incentives. In addition, the plans place different responsibilities on physicians. All of the programs require the primary care physician gatekeeper to be available twenty-four hours a day. In part the provision was included to provide a convenient mechanism for reducing the number of expensive, middle-of-the-night visits to the emergency room. This provision has been quite controversial, however, because it requires primary care physicians to be available to Medicaid patients in a way that they have not been before. In some areas, this strict requirement of twenty-four-hour availability has served as a deterrent to physician participation. Compromise solutions generally allow primary care physicians to pool their availability.

Another important issue for these programs involves the mechanism for reimbursing the primary care physicians. The plans in Kentucky and California have used capitation rates to some extent. These plans set up risk pools of primary care physicians through capitation for some services but bill against these risk pools on a fee-for-service basis for others. The plans in Michigan and Utah are fee-for-service case management systems and do not involve any type of capitation payment to any provider, except to HMOs that function as primary care gatekeepers. In Wayne County, however, primary physicians are paid a case management fee for each enrollee. For reasons similar to those found in other states—mainly, the opposition from the physician community—Michigan and Utah chose not to develop their plans on a prepaid capitation basis. In Wayne County, Michigan, where the medical society sponsored the plan, the members hope to realize cost savings even with a fee-for-service system. In Michigan and Utah, as in other states, plans are likely to gravitate toward capitation after primary care physicians have become accustomed to the gatekeeper role.

In three of the four plans primary care physicians do face some sort of risk, although it is not always a financial one. In Kentucky and California physicians are at financial risk. In Michigan, though, physicians risk reductions in their case management fee and expulsion from the program. The exact nature of the risk sharing in each program is very complicated and is described more completely in each case study.

It is quickly evident that it is difficult to convince physicians to accept a system that makes them risk possible losses, even though the extent of loss is usually limited. Although the Kentucky plan puts physicians at risk for losses, it exempts them from the risk for the first year and then gradually increases their risk over time. Physicians, of course, prefer programs that allow individual primary care physicians to share in the financial profits but not in the financial losses. When physicians are not at risk for financial losses, the losses take the form of professional time for which they may not be reimbursed, but they are not asked to pay money back to the plan.

Each plan pays specialists on a fee-for-service basis, generally using the traditional Medicaid payment levels. In this way, should it be deemed desirable, primary care physicians can be put at risk for payments to specialists by reducing their own capitation payment according to the amount of specialists' fees incurred. Even though many states would like to capitate payment for physicians' services, specialists are hesitant to accept this mode of payment. This reluctance has discouraged states from using capitation because they fear that too few specialists would join to make the plan viable.

The goal of each program is to have primary care physicians have responsibility for enough patients to make the plan viable but not so many that a given provider's practice resembles a "Medicaid mill." Therefore, some of the plans have established minimum and maximum numbers of Medicaid beneficiaries that each provider may enroll. Two of the four plans have chosen to limit the number of patients any provider may serve by refusing to assign additional beneficiaries once the provider has enrolled a certain number. These limits have caused considerable controversy and, in fact, were challenged in a Michigan lawsuit filed by several providers who claimed that the state's limitation severely hindered their ability to earn a living; the court raised the limit. Kentucky implemented its plan at a later date, setting a *guideline* of 1,800 as the maximum number of enrollees per provider. In both Kentucky and California, where programs have enforced a minimum number of enrollees per provider, several physicians have declined to participate because they wanted only to retain the Medicaid patients they were currently serving and did not want to increase their Medicaid patient load. In Kentucky enough primary care physicians were willing to participate, with the condition that they be assigned 300 patients. By way of contrast, Santa Barbara planners had to create a mechanism for pooling risks for physicians who did not wish to enroll the minimum number of patients.

In many instances, hospitals and medical schools have been the traditional providers for Medicaid patients. Primary care network arrangements can have both positive and negative effects on medical school facilities. PCNs can become the central practice focus for residents in primary care specialties, giving them a better orientation to practice, but PCNs generally cost medical schools a substantial amount of money to start. Even so, three of the five medical schools and teaching hospitals in the areas investigated in this study participate in the programs.

Even though the providers in the primary care network programs are predominantly private physicians in solo or group practice, all the sites except Santa Barbara have continued to encourage beneficiaries to enroll in HMOs. In all cases, HMOs are paid on a capitation basis, but they must provide care under the gatekeeping system. In both Michigan and Utah, HMOs have substantially penetrated the Medicaid patient market although, for the most part, they did so before the advent of the primary care network. Although only one HMO in Kentucky and one in Utah have participated in the Medicaid program for a long time, both states would consider contracts with any HMO developed in the future. There are no group or staff models in Santa Barbara, only IPAs, which do not participate and are not being encouraged to participate by the county.

Since one of the major objectives of the primary care network is to control unnecessary and expensive care—for example, inappropriate self-referrals to specialists or inappropriate use of an emergency room—plans must have some means for controlling such events. One such mechanism is to require primary care physicians to authorize a referral to a specialist. Three of the four plans have a referral document that the primary care physician must fill out before a specialist is authorized to treat the patient and the specialist will not be reimbursed without this referral form. Michigan does not use a referral form, but does require that a primary care provider number be obtained over the phone and entered in the appropriate place on the specialist's claim form before reimbursement can be authorized. Most plans have indicated that they would try this approach before implementing a formal written approval system for specialist care.

Hospitals

Reimbursement for hospital care under most plans requires prior authorization, which is also the current Medicaid policy. This requirement seems to be an appropriate and effective means of controlling hospital care. Several of the plans, however, have changed the locus of responsibility for prior authorization away from the state or county government agency to the primary care physician.

In three of the four plans studied, the responsibility for authorizing hospital care lies solely with the primary care physician. Even specialists who wish to admit a patient to the hospital must get prior approval from the primary care physician. The Santa Barbara plan is the only one that does not place the responsibility on the primary care physician. Instead, prior authorization must be obtained from the medical director of the Santa Barbara Health Authority, but only after the primary care physician has already authorized the hospitalization. The original plan in Santa Barbara gave full responsibility for and control over hospitalization to the primary care physician, but the state wanted the county to place stricter regulations on hospitalization.

Most of the experimental projects featuring primary care case management have retained the favorable Medicaid hospital reimbursement rates that states have been able either to negotiate or to mandate through Medicaid programs. Several states, most notably Kentucky, expect they will be able to negotiate an even more favorable discount after their initial experience. Santa Barbara has already negotiated all-inclusive rates similar to the rates negotiated with hospitals under California's selective contracting experiment by the Medi-Cal "czar." Santa Barbara's all-inclusive rate includes the daily room charge as well as ancillary charges and is required to be the same as or less than the rate that would have been negotiated under Medi-Cal's selective contracting program.

None of the programs has attempted to put hospitals at risk for hospital care: no hospital gets paid on a capitation basis. The only financial risk, if any, for hospital care rests with the primary care physician. This is accomplished by interrelating the primary care physician's risk pool with the hospitals in some way. Most hospitals are concerned about the potential of primary care networks to reduce their revenues substantially, although they appear less concerned in the case of Medicaid because Medicaid generally represents a smaller portion of revenues.

Consumer Involvement

Consumers can make valuable contributions in designing or publicizing a plan before it becomes operational. For example, consumers serve on the board of directors in Santa Barbara, a consumer advisory board has been established in Michigan, and consumers in Utah participate through welfare rights groups that have informally contributed to the design of a videotape explaining the plan to recipients. When consumers are excluded from the initial planning stages—as they frequently are—community support is jeopardized, a situation that can lead to lawsuits and make program implementation very difficult. Consumers as well as providers often feel a program is the brainchild of only a few people in the state government who are determined to implement it, regardless of its effect on consumers. Consumers are convinced that if they participated more actively, the implementation would be much smoother.

The 1981 Omnibus Budget Reconciliation Act allows plans qualified for section 2175 waivers to guarantee Medicaid recipients eligibility for up to six months as a way of attracting beneficiaries to the demonstrations and maintaining a stable base of patients for alternative health plans. Although many other experimental programs (most notably the Arizona Health Care Cost Containment System) have found it desirable to offer guaranteed eligibility, no plan described here has implemented such a provision. One reason these plans have not is that three of them are mandatory and do not have to compete with the traditional Medicaid program.

Welfare rights groups, frequently an organized vehicle through which consumers' opinions can be expressed, have actively expressed their grievances under three of the four plans studied (Santa Barbara does not have a welfare rights group). These groups can play important roles by voicing dissatisfaction with various program characteristics; if programs are unresponsive, they can take their grievances to court.

Lawsuits are most often the outcome of unresolved issues concerning access and freedom of choice. It is interesting to note that the two plans unlikely to be involved in lawsuits—Utah and Santa Barbara—involved consumers as an integral part of the planning process.

Utilization Review and Quality Assurance

Utilization review (UR) and quality assurance are two important components of an overall plan, but they are generally neglected until the operational phase of the project. Commonly, also, utilization review is conducted in the absence of any quality-assurance activities.

In all cases, UR responsibility rests with the group administering the plan. In two cases the administrator is the state, and in the other two cases—Kentucky and Santa Barbara—the administrator is an outside fiscal agent. The computer software programs used to monitor utilization patterns are either the Surveillance and Utilization Review

System (SURS) developed for the Medicaid program or one similar to it designed specifically for the experimental program.

In programs where the state or county government is responsible for utilization review, it is usually responsible for quality assurance activities as well—and distinguishing between the two components is often difficult. Rather than doing prospective quality review, states or counties commonly employ an "exceptions" process that identifies aberrant cases through the utilization review system. These cases are then examined as part of the quality-assurance program. Quality assurance in Michigan and Kentucky, however, is the responsibility of the medical society, although both societies have been slow to institute a plan because they do not know how to define norms for detecting underutilization.

Enrollment

The phase-in period is the time the program uses to enroll eligible individuals. Program enrollment in Utah was linked to initial certification or recertification of eligibility, spreading the phase-in period over one year. The phase-in period for the other three programs was relatively short. Some of the programs intended to enroll between 40,000 and 300,000 individuals in only two months, a somewhat unrealistic goal, especially considering the confusion that arises during the enrollment period. Michigan, for example, was successful in enrolling only 38,000 of the 300,000 projected in the first year. When enrollment is tied to recertification, as it was in Utah, individuals can be quickly and efficiently processed after eligibility determination is complete.

The task of enrolling beneficiaries is generally the responsibility of social service and health department workers. Social workers tend to be more knowledgeable about the personal circumstances of Medicaid beneficiaries, whereas health workers are more attuned to the goals and objectives of new health care delivery systems. In addition, social workers occasionally feel that following the plan's guidelines will inconvenience the recipients, so they try to help them by "gaming" the system—for example, by delaying enrollment. Health workers, as the Utah example suggests, understand the programs better and can be quite persuasive in enrolling beneficiaries.

These experimental programs have various means for enrolling beneficiaries in a primary care network. Two of the four enrollment procedures require the Medicaid beneficiary to have a personal interview with the case worker during which the beneficiary chooses one of the participating primary care physicians. Physician selection in

Michigan is made by telephone, and in Santa Barbara selection is made through the mail.

Marketing

Marketing efforts for the mandatory programs have focused on informing beneficiaries about the plan and about enrollment procedures. Marketing a voluntary program is more difficult, since the goal is to attract beneficiaries to an alternative delivery system and away from the free choice of provider under Medicaid. The programs have generally been advertised through the mail and at community meetings that reportedly have not been well attended. These methods do not seem to have had much effect on enrollment. Beneficiaries usually wait until they get sick before they select a primary care physician, and then they are frequently assigned a physician at random. Since the physician to whom they are assigned is not always conveniently located, they frequently seek care from a physician to whom they have not been assigned and then become dissatisfied with the system. Furthermore, the system becomes burdened with problems resulting from denial of payment for unauthorized care.

All plans send information to beneficiaries through the mail, and administrators have learned that such mailings should be easily distinguished from other health or welfare department mailings so that the beneficiaries will not disregard the information. Even under the best circumstances, it seems unreasonable to expect more than 35 to 40 percent enrollment after an initial mailing.